THE LANGUAGE OF
LEADERSHIP

Dr. Marlene Caroselli

Published by   Human Resource Development Press, Inc.
             22 Amherst Road
             Amherst, Massachusetts 01002

For information about our audio products, write us at:
Newbridge Book Clubs, 3000 Cindel Drive, Delran, NJ   08370

ISBN No. 0-87425-130-3

First Printing, March, 1990

Cover Design by Nelda Jansen, Old Mill Graphics

Word Processing by Susan Kotzin

Editing by Lisa Wood

Photograph by Sandi Kantor

To my family: leaders and linguists all

TABLE OF CONTENTS

PREFACE

Like many people, I have long been fascinated with leaders and leadership. Leaders themselves are intriguing topics of study, but equally interesting are the circumstances that propelled them to assume control over the lives of others. Their paths to leadership are varied and circuitous and sometimes selected for them, rather than by them. Ultimately, though, each leader arrives at a place where he or she is in a superior position, from which it is easy to see what needs to be done.

Equally fascinating to me is language. I became lost in a dictionary as a child and—not ever wishing to find my way out—wound up an instructor of English. Writing a book about language was simply a question of following my way along the path destiny had selected for me.

The Language of Leadership is the natural result of these two fascinations. When I began my research, I found a good many books in the area of leadership, but none devoted exclusively to the language employed by leaders. Similarly, I could find numerous books on the broad topic of language, but none that dealt entirely with the way leaders use words, how they forge them into verbal chains with which they captivate their followers and inspire them to accomplish goals for a cause, a cause in which leaders and followers alike believe. My intent was to meld these two areas so that the reader could become more of a leader by incorporating into his or her language the elements of leadership language displayed by some of our most notable figures.

When I submitted an advance chapter to Judy Columbus, the subject of Chapter Six, she responded, "You have blended several elements in a way I have not seen before, and in a most readable and integrated fashion. In one text, the reader finds a critique of writing styles, references to historically wise authors, content worth the reading and a call to action. I particularly enjoy your making the reader other than passive, by inviting his participation throughout. The ready student could learn to read, write and think, all in one place."

She captured my intent completely. The book not only analyzes the language of ten prominent Americans, it also provides ways for the reader to practice applying the analyzed components to his or her own style of communicating. (Two and a half decades of teaching have left me reluctant to make a point without showing others how they could profit from it.) Should you, the reader, wish further instruction on either an individual or corporate basis, you may write me at the Center for Professional Development; 10305 Summertime Lane; Culver City, California 90230.

ACKNOWLEDGMENTS

To the leaders who consented to have their language examined in this book, I extend my gratitude. Lee Iacocca, Mario Cuomo, Tom Peters, Peter Drucker, Judith Bardwick, Judy Columbus, Barbara Henry, Kitty Carlisle Hart and Pat Russell—without them, there would have been no book.

A special word of thanks must go to my aunt, Elizabeth DeLucia, who put me in touch with Governor Mario Cuomo. It was his address to the Democratic National Convention that was the genesis of this book.

To my sister, Trish Caroselli Rintels, I am especially indebted. She nurtured the manuscript (and its author) from conception to completion. Writing is a lonely pursuit, and without her, I would undoubtedly have become too insular. She brought balance and patience and companionship to this lonely pursuit in which I immersed myself for a two-year period.

Finally, to my publisher, Robert W. Carkhuff, who had faith in this book when the concept was merely an embryo, I thank you for believing in me. You never, not for a moment, doubted that this book would become a successful reality.

Marlene Caroselli
Los Angeles, California

CHAPTER ONE:
An Overview of Leadership

Introduction

Language—that wondrous construct of symbols that we use to communicate with one another and with ourselves. Our language, whether we are using it verbally or nonverbally, is the vehicle we employ to reach out to one another. Think for a moment how difficult, if not impossible, it would be to live without communicating. Even if you are not speaking or writing with words, you are still communicating via the clothes you wear, the car you drive, the way you decorate your environment, the friends you choose—and all of these reveal information about you and the way that you lead your life.

In addition to this "object language," there is the language expressed by your body. Raised eyebrows, a hand to your mouth, a circle formed by your thumb and forefinger: all convey meaning through physical gestures instead of words. And body language not only speaks as loudly as words, but more frequently than words, in the opinion of many experts in this field of kinesics.

What about silences? Depending upon the circumstances, silence can relay many possible emotions: anger, fear, reverence, respect, to name but a few. As sentient beings, capable of receiving sensory impressions and translating them into relevant expressions of ourselves, we take those thoughts, ideas, impressions and images which flood into our brains (at a speed of 800 a minute) and we transform them into statements (verbal or nonverbal) which have significance for others and for ourselves. Even the way we use our voices to put forth our verbal messages is a kind of language unto itself.

"Paralanguage" is the use of vocal characteristics to convey meaning beyond the words themselves. In your mind, speak the name of a friend to show (through various tones and inflections) that you are angry...surprised...doubting. The word is the same word each time, but the voice can bring several new interpretations to the utterances of that name.

As fascinating as the study of nonverbal language is, we shall concentrate in this book on the study of words alone. We shall examine intently those symbols of language that tell others who we are and what we believe; and who, what, and how we love. Our verbal symbols serve as the nexus bridging thought and actions, imaginings and reality, dreams and deeds.

We encode our fears and our hopes, our desires and our needs into words. These spoken and written symbols form a cultural network of understanding. In both our microcosmic and our macrocosmic societies, words have meanings that the society has agreed upon. With this commonality in operation, we can use words and be reasonably assured they will have significance for those who read and hear them.

We turn to words to help us clarify our thoughts, define our intentions, acquire our knowledge. Words cause us pain, they evoke anger, they make us hate, they lead us to war. But they also make us laugh, bring us joy, and satisfy our emotional hungers. They challenge us to be more than we are, to work harder than we do, to reach established goals. Words, in short, have power.

Leadership Traits

Leaders understand the power of language; they employ the language of power. Leaders use words to win the innumerable small battles which constitute the essence of our days upon this earth. Leaders understand that words can be wooed and won. If we are willing to sustain that courtship, we can be assured success in virtually all our endeavors.

Words are our tools for personal success. Whether you are requesting a raise, or negotiating a deal, or making a presentation, or applying for a job, you are depending on words to get the message across clearly and convincingly.

Verbal bridges are built between the leader and his followers. The leader forays into the domain of his followers, uses words to convince them of the correctness of his vision, and persuades them to follow him back across the bridge into his own domain, a domain of ideas waiting to be realized.

Since a leader could not be a leader without followers, it is important to examine what a leader does to convince others to follow her back across that verbal bridge. To be sure, leaders lead by example; they exhibit certain behaviors, evince certain traits. And, they share certain common qualities as far as their linguistic style is concerned.

During the 1800's, with the influx of immigrants from Europe, leaders were thought to be born and not made, largely because of their birth into noble and/or wealthy families.

But in a democratic nation such as ours, that notion soon lost favor, and researchers began to examine the traits separating leaders from nonleaders. The social scientists could not agree, however, on specific traits that were common to all leaders.

Contemporary leadership theorists are returning to the trait theory of leadership; they are finding that certain demonstrable qualities are shared by leaders. Among those qualities are the following. (Which ones do you associate with yourself?)

Develops teams

A leader who develops teams and team spirit will constantly support team members. Like a coach, she shouts support for the winning moves of her team members. But she also cheers the team on when there is a lag in "scoring." The team developer, in both the actual and the metaphoric sense, creates a cohesive team spirit to support the individual members engaged in an undertaking. She rallies a group on to victory by virtue of her ability to verbalize faith and enthusiasm. She uses language to lead.

The team developer realizes that at times the leadership "torch" must be passed on to others. This empowerment of others serves a dual purpose; it helps them hone their own team-building skills and it brings a fresh approach, perhaps even a special expertise, to the group's efforts.

With the current emphasis in American corporations on Total Quality Management, it is especially important that team members engage in open communication with others and that they contribute to group problem-solving. The team developer is committed to bringing unity to groups so they can achieve common goals more readily.

The team developer reflects the following in her language:

- receptivity to the opinions of others in the team
- concern over solutions to, rather than causers of, the problem
- positive input, leading to efficient group decision-making
- analysis (but not condemnation) of breakdowns in the group's efficient operation.
- nonevaluative commentary
- control over conflicts
- reminders of what the overarching goals are.

The leader takes a sincere interest in the progress of her supporters. At various times, as a developer, she encourages them, nurtures them to a fuller realization of their abilities, pushes them forward. When you help a friend by listening to his problems, or work with a colleague on a project, you demonstrate leadership skills if you are encouraging others to give their best, to do their best.

The leader is a gardener who plants seeds of championship potential and then waits for them to blossom. The soil, of course, must be rich with verbal and other nutrients.

Energizes

The leader brings a strong sense of purpose to her work. Her enthusiasm is apparent in the way she "attacks" the project before her. Her unbridled fervor is usually not constrained by hurdles or setbacks. The leader who has energy for a task usually manages to energize others as well.

Think about a project or a hobby that so consumes you that you lose all sense of time. We seem to forget the world when an interesting assignment captures our interest or engages our mind. Leaders who are committed to carrying out a mission have a fire burning inside them, a consuming passion which relegates other concerns to second place. Leaders ignite others, through their enthusiasm and through their energy, to participate in the drive toward goal accomplishment.

The leader may not be in perfect physical condition—Franklin D. Roosevelt, for example, was confined to a wheelchair for much of his presidency and John F. Kennedy suffered from constant back pain—but they are strong enough to contribute energy and vitality. The leader who is frequently fatigued, suffering from a serious medical condition, or unable to cope with the effects of stress simply cannot lend a dynamic thrust to an undertaking for a sustained period.

Shares knowledge

We expect our leaders to be intelligent, to know more than we know, to possess an expertise greater than our own. When this is not the case, we become disillusioned and feel somehow cheated. Often without question, we will follow someone who is better than we, but when we find chinks in the leader's intellectual armor, we resent and often resist his efforts.

While leaders, as they ascend in their careers, must become more generalist than specialist, they should be acquiring new skills all of the time. And, they should be making subordinates aware of these skills. Otherwise, dissatisfaction among the rank and file may turn to subversion.

Once followers begin to think, "I can do that better than he is doing it," they begin to find reasons not to cooperate. The wise leader admits he cannot be an expert in everything but he can be an expert at leading—and that is usually what he is being paid to do.

Motivates

Leaders believe in what they are doing. They are caught up in the energy generated by pursuing a project in which they are interested. They are enamored of their work. When real estate developer Trammel Crow, for example, was asked the secret of his success, he replied, "Love." We do best what we love doing, and the leader's enthusiasm invariably spills over and magnetizes the interest of his followers. Our ability to articulate that love enables us to motivate others.

A century ago, John Dewey observed that children learn best when they are interested in a subject. (Weren't your highest grades in those courses you enjoyed the most?) The same is true of learners or problem tacklers today. We do best when we have a sincere interest in a subject.

With his words, the leader is able to share his fascination in a pursuit; in so doing, he ignites the imagination of his followers, making them eager to learn more about the pursuit. Supervisors often complain about "unmotivated" people, but the truth is, we are *all* motivated. We may not be motivated to do what the supervisor wants, but we *are* motivated to accomplish certain goals. The trick for the leader is to use language in such a way that followers are motivated to accomplish the goals which the leader feels are critical for the organization's success.

The motivator helps his followers understand the passion he feels for a given undertaking. In time, ideally, that passion will lead to precision on the part of others. As they become more and more involved in a pursuit, they become self-directed. "Romance," as Alfred North Whitehead opined, "precedes precision."

Think about something you do very well: designing a computer program or writing a report or playing tennis. Now trace back to the time when you first took an interest in that particular field. Didn't romance precede your precision? Often, our fascination for a subject begins with an introduction to the subject by someone with a deep-rooted enthusiasm. That person may have led you to your own enthusiasm by way of words which promised wonder and discovery.

It is not enough to be energized by a new idea; the leader must energize others in order for change to occur. Spreading the metaphoric fire of conviction is a matter of lighting up the hearts and minds of followers by setting the match of inspired language to the fuel of potential.

When we convince others to do what we feel is best, we must depend on the force of our words. Being persuasive entails being ethical, if the leader is using his leadership skills according to the definition of leadership we subscribe to. Leadership language is an instrument for making good things happen—good for us, good for others, and especially, good for the organization.

The leader/motivator begins to make good things happen by aiding others to develop an interest in the task at hand. She then provides goal information by

- being specific about expectations
- providing information about the contribution the team can make
- supporting team members and instilling confidence in them
- continually providing feedback about their work
- recognizing their efforts.

The leader discovers excellence—in herself, in her undertakings, in her colleagues. It is not enough, however, to recognize the efforts of just a few. The leader shares information about those individual endeavors which contribute to team success, thereby inspiring others to similar action.

Just as the captain of a sports team can make the team more successful by identifying the unique skills of each player and making each player feel he or she is an important part of the team, so, too, does the motivational leader employ words to give praise, to express appreciation, and to bring significance to individuals whose work might otherwise go unnoticed.

As individuals, we each deserve to be treated with respect and dignity. In turn, it is hoped we bring that consideration to others and even to the work we do. The leader as motivator does not hesitate to compliment the efforts of the "little guy"; she does not hesitate to compliment a janitor or thank a gas station attendant. Motivating, if done properly, becomes a natural part of one's leadership style.

Investigates

The leader who develops and motivates team members needs information about individual performers and performances to make the operation run more smoothly. Think about the instructor who stands behind a podium for a full hour or who sits at a desk and corrects papers. Such a person seldom arouses excitement. The lecturer who walks around, by comparison, lends a vitality to the learning situation. His very presence bespeaks a concern for what is happening.

Similarly, in a corporate context, the difference between dull and dynamic can often be attributed to one factor: investigation. Getting out of the office and into the midst of others' activities allows employees to see that management is taking a real interest in the contributions made by individuals and teams. Those managers who take the time to find out what is really happening among the rank and file of the organization will gain insights and information that could have been obtained in no other way.

The leader is hungry for accomplishment; his desire for making the world (or at least *his* world) a better place is so strong that it can be likened to hunger. That hunger is translated into words, at the very beginning of the project, to ensure that the goal is clarified enough so others can commit to it.

The investigator asks questions. He, through his words and actions, is able to find both the problems and the promise of his followers.

It is one thing for a leader to have an "open-door policy" and hope that subordinates will walk through the door eager to share information. It is quite another thing, though, to assist those unwilling to come through the door by going out to meet them and investigate what is really happening. The leader who is willing to discuss, to probe beneath the surface, to get—through his discussions and meetings—a true sense of what needs to be dealt with is the leader who will win the respect of his followers.

Enlivens

Consider all the instructors and superiors you have encountered thus far in your life. Which ones stand out in your mind? Usually it is those who have a flair for the dramatic, who enliven learning and living and working by bringing a sense of the dramatic to rather pedestrian situations. For example, a young man in a *Fortune 500* organization was asked by his boss to give a presentation on time management to his peers.

To illustrate the point that we need to have schedules and adhere to them, he deliberately entered the conference room five minutes late. He rushed in wearing a jogging suit and sneakers and apologized for his tardiness while peeling off his "sweats" to reveal his business suit underneath. Upon conclusion of his speech—to make his point all over again—he flew out of the conference room, pulling on his jogging outfit as he ran, and breathlessly explaining that he was late for another meeting.

His dramatic entrance and exit made his points about time management really come to life.

Not everyone, of course, is prone to histrionic behavior. But certainly all of us can find ways to bring a bit of humor or poignancy or celebration to ordinary events on ordinary days.

To do so is to recognize the importance of drama in the leader's behavior and the need for it in the followers' environment. These special people, these soul-stirring "enliveners" make the mundane aspects of our lives memorable. They celebrate living, using their words to bring life into a sharper focus.

Organizes

The leader not only controls, directs, and plans the activities of others, he also assumes responsibility for organizing: people, paper, places, projects and time. Ever mindful of the "Five P's for Success:" Proper Planning Prevents Poor Performance, the organized leader begins by analyzing current practices to determine where waste is occurring.

The leader does not waste his time, nor does he waste the time of other people. To maximize effort and to make efforts most valuable, the leader organizes in order to accomplish goals more easily.

He delegates rather than dumps, he analyzes before asking, he eliminates the unnecessary and/or obsolete.

Is mature

The effective leader is one whose self-confidence results in the attainment of long-range goals. Not needing immediate gratification, the effective manager is emotionally stable and so can concentrate on the needs of others. Not preoccupied with draining emotions such as jealousy, anger, insecurity or suspicion, the leader communicates goal-attainment rather than self-aggrandizement. He is sensitive to the needs of others and can encourage when he sees doubt beginning to permeate spirits. Willing to anticipate problems and knowing how unpredictable life can be, the leader will build contingency plans into his short-term and long-term strategies.

Additionally, the leader maintains control of himself; he does not yield to petty or self-indulgent behavior. His judgments are sound and he knows how to separate the trivial from the valuable. Whether dealing with unpleasant situations or unpleasant people, the leader serves as an exemplar and accepts the weight of being a role model. The organizational pacesetter is willing to take calculated risks and willing to face the consequences when those risks prove to have been the wrong choices.

Is self-confident

The leader views himself in a positive light, unabashedly admitting what he can do well and determined to use his talents to bring about positive change. After all, if the leader does not have faith in himself, how can he expect his followers to? The leader is honest about his abilities, willing to experiment, and able to continue moving toward a goal, even when things do not go exactly as planned.

To quote Lee Iacocca:

If your top executives don't have some ego drive, how will your company stay stirred up and competitive? There's a world of difference between a strong ego, which is essential, and a large ego—which can be destructive. The guy with a strong ego knows his own strengths. He's confident. He has a realistic idea of what he can accomplish, and he moves purposefully toward his goal. But the guy with a large ego is always looking for recognition. He constantly needs to be patted on the back. He thinks he's a cut above everybody else. And he talks down to the people who work for him.[1]

Leaders recognize human potential. They know people can do so much more than they ask themselves to do. It is said Einstein felt he was only using a quarter of his total brain power; scientists calculate that the average person employs only one to ten percent of his or her brain's capability.

Cognizant of the power each of us has to make things happen, leaders tap into that power. If we believe we are going to fail at an attempt, really believe that, then there is no point in making the attempt. We must have faith, the leader assures us, that what we are doing has at least some chance of succeeding.

Leaders are not foolish optimists but rather, realistic optimists who hope for the best and work hard to present themselves and their followers in the best possible light. Recognizing that things do not always turn out as he wished and planned, the leader nonetheless has implicit conviction in the creative power of the people to bring about a change for the better.

Is ethical

We rightfully expect that our leaders will demonstrate a high ethical sense, that they will be honest in their dealings and that they will exhibit honor and trustworthiness as they interact with others on behalf of the organization.

Leaders have a sense of social responsibility. They are concerned with improving the quality of life for many people—not just themselves. In a well-known study of derailed executives, the Center for Creative Leadership found that integrity was indeed an important word to successful executives.

Leaders keep an open mind; they try to avoid rigid, stereotypical thinking. They realize a given situation might be interpreted in various ways by various people and they try to listen carefully to all sides of an issue. Often the situation calls for approaching a problem from multiple angles and finding truth as a result of not accepting only the first impression. As an illustration, look at the following picture. Do you see an old woman, a young woman, or both?

Part of that ethical stance requires leaders to be honest with themselves about themselves. They assess themselves constantly. Their weaknesses are either ignored, compensated for, or converted to strengths, if necessary. As part of their self-evaluation, leaders ascertain what skills are needed for the successful accomplishment of a mission.

Leaders do not know everything and do not pretend to. They focus on what they *can* contribute, thereby validating Peter Drucker's observation that no one has ever accused the world famous violinist Jascha Heifetz of not being able to play the trumpet.

Envisions

Leadership is usually defined as achieving desired results through the efforts of others. To the extent that you can influence others to do what you believe is right and necessary for your organization, you will derive satisfaction from your job and will be regarded as a leader.

The ability to create, to envision a dream and to reify it by sharing that vision with others is a critical element of managerial success. The leader makes things happen by creating something out of nothing. She employs language to help capture the imagination of her followers, to inspire them to share her vision of what might be. Through well-articulated statements, the leader stimulates others to action, catching them up in the belief that something new and different and better can occur. In short, she influences.

Through well-chosen words, the leader is able to inspire others with the vision she has of future success. Just as athletic coaches lead their teams to victory with continual descriptions of what victory will be like, so do other leaders seek to take charge by forming visions of success in the minds of their followers.

When Robert Kennedy remarked, "Some people look at the present and ask, 'Why?' I look at the future and ask 'Why not?'", he was creating a vision, a hope of the future for others to be inspired by. Leaders "see" their success long before it actually happens and so are willing to engage in mental rehearsal, just as Olympic athletes do before their actual performances.

Without hesitation, the leader seeks to unite her followers by forging a common bond, a mutually agreed-upon concept of their shared mission. She is able to fashion order out of chaos by stripping away nonessential information. Next, she hews a pristine image, a clear direction. Since the leader always knows where she is going, her followers have no doubt they, too, are on the path to accomplishing their mission.

Follows through

It is not enough for the leader to have a vision—the leader must also follow through on the vision to ensure it gestates and is born. Because the leader is intent on following his goals by taking all the necessary and practical steps required, others are likely to follow his plans. Trust is established when the leader is viewed as a visionary who is willing to work hard so embryonic goals can be delivered.

Generally speaking, followers will not commit themselves for very long to a leader who is not also a pragmatist. As most of us have discovered, dreams are only powerful when we believe they can come true. Pipe dreams belong in the realm of fantasy; leaders' dreams belong in the realm of possibility.

We pledge our trust to those individuals who can make things happen. As followers, we need to believe that the leader's actions will actually have an impact upon us, will affect us in some significant way. If we do not believe that the outcome of the leader's efforts will have any impact upon us or upon our immediate environment, we are not likely to follow that person. It is only when we tie our fate in with the leader's that we can be said to be following him.

Part of that tie-in depends on the sharing of power, and power can take many shapes. Information is one kind of power. Keeping recruits aware of the leader's intent makes them better equipped to achieve organizational aims.

Similarly, we must feel that the leader can be trusted to follow through on articulated plans. Should the leader's behavior or words differ radically from what we have come to expect from him, we would be less inclined to follow him. We seek constancy and predictability and sincerity from our leaders; we need to see congruency between their words and their actions if we are to trust them.

Communicates

The leader has a unique ability to make his followers loyal supporters through lexical and syntactical artistry. (We will see specific examples of this artistry in our examination of the words of various leaders in the chapters which follow.) The leader chooses—from the million words available to him—the ones that best depict his message; he finds the lexical symbols that best convey his convictions.

The leader's words are structured to help his audience conceptualize, to force them to think new thoughts or to pursue new challenges. So often the leader will lead others from the abstract to the specific by way of concrete comparisons. He will also select language that is simple, direct, and familiar in order to establish trust.

"Big men use little words," Winston Churchill asserted. When we think about the leaders who have most inspired us, we usually find them articulating profound thought with little words. "I have a dream," Martin Luther King revealed. John F. Kennedy brought forth an era of Peace Corps altruism when he exhorted, "Ask not what your country can do for you; ask what you can do for your country."

Words have been compared to sunbeams: the more they are focused and condensed, the deeper they burn. The words that are burned into our memory cells are the words which we can easily recall.

If our words are to be remembered, we must choose words that are memorable. Use your dictionary if needed to "translate" the following hard-to-remember ideas. (The answers can be found at the end of this chapter.)

1. Deleterious consequences often ensue from accelerated execution.

2. Should an equestrian entity be made available to you without expectation of reimbursement, refrain from making an ocular foray into the oral cavity of that entity.

3. Sagacity dictates that one not excise the proboscis as a punitive measure against one's personal visage.

4. Do not traverse an edifice erected to afford passage over an aqueous mass until the temporal eventuality is imminent.

5. It is not advantageous to garner the totality of one's gallinaceous collections into a singular receptacle made of pliant twigs.

6. Lexical truncations, abbreviations or similar condensations can be equated to the quintessence or very spiritual embodiment of persiflage.

7. It is experiential activities of an amorous nature which bear the responsibility for the causality of the mundane entity progressing along an axial trajectory.

8. A singular graphic representation is more meritorious than philological expressions comprised of that figure which occupies the position four to the left of the decimal point in the Arabic notation.

9. The very deprivation of a physical entity or the temporal and spatial separation from that entity is often the cause of amplification of an amorous affinity.

A communicator who is able to share her vision with clarity and precision carefully avoids "doublespeak"—a portmanteau amalgam, created by joining the words, "doublethink" and "newspeak" from

George Orwell's novel *1984*. A would-be leader's failure to deal honestly with issues may lead to doublespeak expressions such as the following.

Can you match the terms[2] on the left with their actual meanings on the right? (The answers can be found at the end of this chapter.)

1.	safety-related occurrence	A.	to smell something
2.	incomplete success	B.	used car
3.	fiscal underachievers	C.	pig pens and chicken coops
4.	service technician	D.	thermometer
5.	non-goal-oriented member of society	E.	bank robbery
6.	single purpose agricultural structures	F.	newspaper delivery person
7.	downsizing personnel	G.	accident
8.	advanced downward adjustments	H.	budget cuts
9.	collateral damage	I.	frightened
10.	experienced automobile	J.	street person
11.	media courier	K.	greeting cards
12.	unauthorized withdrawal	L.	failure
13.	digital fever computer	M.	repairman
14.	conduct an organoleptic analysis	N.	civilian casualties of war
15.	philosophically disillusioned	O.	grocery-store checkout clerk
16.	nail technician	P.	antisatellite weapon
17.	kinetic kill vehicle	Q.	the poor
18.	ultimate high-intensity warfare	R.	firing employees
19.	social-expression products	S.	manicurist
20.	career associate scanning professional	T.	nuclear war

Think about someone you regard as a leader. What is his language like? Does he "doublespeak?" Consider Lee Iacocca's comments about the leader as communicator:

> It's important to talk to people in their own language. If you do it well, they'll say, "God, he said exactly what I was thinking." And when they begin to respect you, they'll follow you to the death.[3]

Talking to people in their own language often means using humor appropriately. The pressures of everyday life, the inevitable strains that are put upon any relationship, the obligations we must fulfill as employees, as members of a family, as members of larger social structure—all these potential stresses can be lightened if we maintain the ability to laugh at ourselves and at our situations. The sharp edge of diurnal events can be dulled by finding the humorous moments and sharing them.

Actualizes

In the process of self-actualizing, the leader is becoming "all that he can be," to paraphrase a popular advertisement. He is following a dream and leading others to follow it with him. As the dream becomes actualized, so do the dreamers.

The leader/dreamer is committed to a mission and will take whatever steps are necessary to meet his objectives. This sense of total commitment can be found in the words of Vince Lombardi, former coach of the Green Bay Packers: "Every time a football player goes out to ply his trade, he's got to play from the ground up—from the soles of his feet right up to his head. Some guys play with their heads, and sure, you need to be smart to be number one in anything you try. But most important, you've got to play with your heart. If you're lucky enough to find a guy with a lot of head and a lot of heart, he'll never come off the field second."

The leader is committed—with both head and heart—to effecting a future that represents the amelioration of an existing state. Undaunted by a particular failure, or even multiple failures, leaders continue to move along, learning as they go. They never lose sight of that future condition and consequently view failure as only a temporary state of being.

Is intelligent

Leaders make valuable contributions to their organizations precisely because they have refined their thinking skills to view situations from both a long-range and a more immediate perspective. Many leaders also actively seek to become lateralized in their thinking: to develop both left-brain proficiency and right-brain creativity.

An example of this type of bimodality would be the person who engages in "Janusian" thinking—derived from Janus, the Roman god after whom the month of January is named. Janus is featured on Roman coins with two faces. They are looking simultaneously forward and backward, which is what the month of January does: recognizes the end of the old year and looks forward to the new year at the same time.

When you think in Janusian terms, you are able to effectively combine opposite ideas into a workable premise. In dialectical terms, it is like taking a thesis, joining it with its opposite or antithesis and winding up with a synthesis or merged whole.

One aspect of leaders' intelligence involves the constant quest for improvement. Leaders use their communication skills to learn about flaws in a system or process or operation; they then seek ways to eliminate those flaws so efforts can be maximized.

Another aspect involves their liberal attitude towards ideas other than their own. They welcome divergent thoughts, avoid a total dependence on convergent thinking, and display their receptivity to others' suggestions by recognizing rather than ridiculing.

On a related note, leaders seem to have a high tolerance for ambiguity. Recognizing that the brain does not work in a completely linear fashion, leaders demonstrate a comfort with the chaos of exploding ideas, many of them seemingly unrelated to the stimulus that caused them. These exploding ideas often represent a challenge to the leader: can she bring order out of these ideas which have been causing a "storm" in her brain?

The leader depends on analysis and rational thought, it is true, but such thinking may actually be a deterrent to the leader if it leads her to over-analyze. Progress may in fact be impeded if the leader is only following logical dictates. Sometimes the "irrational" drives are necessary to spur herself and others on to greater heights.

Ambition is such a drive, the desire to be first when being second would probably, rationally, not be much different from being first. Excessive examination along these lines might cool the fires of our drive; the cold process of inquiry should not be permitted to make tepid the desire to succeed in a leadership position.

Unlike the cold process of inquiry, the creative process contains heat. To create something where nothing existed before, to look at the ordinary and see the extraordinary, to mold the unusual out of the usual—these terse descriptions of the creative process reflect an integral aspect of leadership: the ability to bring about change and persuade others to participate in the process.

While invention or creativity or artistry can certainly be an individual pursuit, the leader does not work in isolation beyond a certain point. Instead, he engages followers who will support the new concept and see it to fruition.

Welcomes change

The leader creates action where there was none; in so doing, she must be sensitive to the needs and feelings of others and must realize that by creating action she is also creating change. And change is bound to disrupt.

Stimulated by a concept or a cause, the leader is usually quite willing to take risks, to display the firmness or courage that is often required if she is to defend and protect her idea. To make an idea a reality is a long and often difficult process. It is never easy to introduce change to others, and courage is frequently required if the leader is to carry through on the change action. Sometimes, she must take risks if she is to alter events or improve environments. The careful risk-taker will work to lead her followers to her way of thinking, which includes welcoming change.

The leader knows people resist change out of fear (usually of the unknown), perceived threats to self-esteem, economic concerns, inconvenience, and the disruption of established patterns.

Leaders themselves do not resist change, for they know that life and lives are in a constant state of flux. Nothing remains permanent. Those who are most ready to deal with life's emergencies are those who have anticipated many possible outcomes and have made provisions for them.

Think about the last time you tried to introduce change to a group. Do you recall the reactions of the people who would be most affected by the change? Did you find yourself having to defend your position? Were you, perhaps, nervous about the risk you were taking, worried the effort involved might be in vain? When we speak about having the courage of our convictions, we are speaking of the need to stand firm on an issue to which we are committed, despite the controversy or resistance it might engender.

With firmness, the leader seeks to assure followers that since we cannot control the changes life brings to individuals and to organizations, we should strive to control the correlates of change. Such correlates would include the degree of our own preparedness, knowledge of technological advances, or familiarity with various approaches or strategies for dealing with the changes which accompany change.

The leader is a language master who uses encouraging, comforting words to begin the change process: she begins to melt away or unfreeze the old habits, old thinking, old procedures. Bit by bit, she thaws the solidity of the former way of doing things so that she can introduce the necessary change. At the appropriate time, when fears have been allayed and explanations have been given, she introduces the change and supports its implementation.

Her next step is to solidify this change and to make *it* the norm, until such time as another change is imminent and the whole process must begin again.

THE CHANGE PROCESS

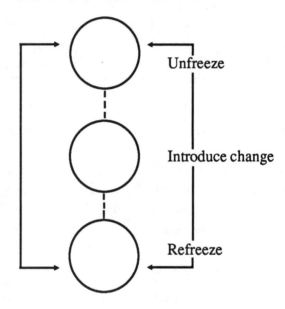

Unfreeze

Introduce change

Refreeze

The leader takes steps to ensure the change will be handled fairly, with a minimum of emotional and physical disturbance. The best way to introduce change is with no surprises. The leader's followers or team members should be prepared for the change well in advance. As a leader, you should handle all questions and concerns carefully, no matter how trivial they may seem.

Whether you are dealing with one person or with a group, your followers deserve to be fully informed about the reason for the change. It is incumbent upon you to make the transition from the old way to the new way as smooth as possible. Do this by helping the individual(s) concerned to acquire the tools needed to handle change well.

To summarize then, let us say that today's leader exhibits most, if not all, of the behaviors shown in this illustration.

LEADERSHIP BEHAVIORS

develops teams
energizes
shares knowledge
motivates

is self-confident
is ethical
envisions
follows through

The leader is one who

investigates
enlivens
organizes
is mature

communicates
actualizes
is intelligent
welcomes change

Leadership Styles

When there is a leader to unify the disparate views, styles, and values of group members, the group will work more efficiently. Many leaders operate with a preferred style of leadership, the most typical of which can be classified as follows.

Autocratic

Most of us can recall an instructor or coach or boss or drill sergeant who was a stern taskmaster indeed. Such individuals exert a strong influence over their charges and often manage, as a result, to have their groups perform excellent work. But there is sometimes a price to be paid for the outstanding results achieved by the autocrat's group. Like the drill sergeant who is able to get his or her recruits to form a cohesive, well-disciplined unit, the autocrat does get results, but often at the expense of group harmony or genuine concern for feelings.

Paradoxically, it is usually many years after such a person has been part of our lives that we are able to view him or her with respect and appreciation. While we might not have approved of the autocrat's behavior when we were directly influenced by it, we often say afterwards, "He was tough, but I learned a lot from him."

Laissez-faire

Literally, this french expression means "let [them] do [as they wish]." The laissez-faire style of leadership is essentially a leaderless style, since the leader virtually abdicates his role of being in charge and allows subordinates to make their own decisions and solve their own problems as much as they can. If the project is not especially important or if the group members are particularly skilled, this style will work well. As a rule, though, productivity declines when groups do not have the guidance of a firm leader.

Democratic or Participative

When the leader is secure enough and when time allows, the democratic leadership style works well. Because group members are encouraged to contribute their ideas, they often feel a real sense of belonging; they thrive on knowing their contributions are valued. Consequently, the work produced under a democratic leader is usually superior in quality.

STYLES OF LEADERSHIP

Autocratic Laissez-faire Democratic

SITUATIONAL LEADERSHIP

The democratic style does not work in every circumstance, nor is it as efficient as the autocratic style, but it does engender an *esprit de corps* among participants.

Situational

Situational leadership depends on a number of different factors. As the term suggests, the leader's behavior will change, depending upon the situation she is facing. Rather than conform to, and depend exclusively on, one of the three traditional styles shown above, the situational leader will operate selectively.

Depending upon the nature of the task and the nature of her group, the situational leader will modify her typical behavior and select whichever one of the three basic styles will best match the forces in the situation.

The perceptive leader will assess the makeup of the group and will select a leadership approach that aligns her control of the group with the group's need to be controlled. When the group is solidly behind the leader *or* when the group is quite divisive, the leader can and should exert authority. When the task to be accomplished is either very structured or very unstructured, the leader will find that an emphasis on task rather than on people is what is needed to get the job done.

A more democratic approach (even leaning toward the laissez-faire style) can be employed if the group is moderately "controllable" and if the task is moderately structured.

Power and Leadership

In the next chapter, you will learn about the leader's use of power in interpersonal communications. Unfortunately, in the minds of many people, the word "power" has come to have Machiavellian overtones. Historically, America is a nation which has rebelled against power. We cherish our independence and will go to great lengths to prevent any one figure from acquiring too much power.

Until only recently, we have looked upon the power-hungry with disfavor. (Megalomania, after all, is a mental disorder.) Most of us have associated power-users with unscrupulous, self-serving individuals who manipulate others in order to achieve their own ends.

But current research is showing that true leaders enjoy using their power and are comfortable with it—so comfortable, in fact, that they don't mind sharing that control when it is appropriate to do so.

Most leaders are not malevolent figures, but rather creators of action who depend on others, and who are depended upon *by* others, to make things happen in an organization.

Writing in the *Harvard Business Review,*[4] John Kotter exhorts us to rethink the connotations we have long related to power:

> From my own observations, I suspect that a large number of managers—especially the young, well-educated ones—perform significantly below their potential because they do not understand the dynamics of power and because they have not nurtured and developed the instincts needed to effectively acquire and use power.

Yes, power can be used for selfish purposes. And leadership can be used to do irreparable harm to others. But, throughout this book, we stress the use of leadership and of power to bring about positive change.

Position power

Using only the power of your position will not work for very long, Kotter believes.[5] For one thing, there will inevitably be some individuals on whom you depend who are not directly under your control. Secondly, most people will not take orders continuously and unquestioningly simply because you are the boss.

Persuasion power

Admittedly, persuasion is important in getting others to do what we want them to do. However, Kotter also specifies the disadvantages of persuasive attempts: they take considerable time, they require the persuader to have extensive knowledge, and they may not be well-received.[6]

If position power and persuasion power have drawbacks for the leader seeking to be successful in his efforts to bring about organizational change, how then can the manager/leader cope with his dependence on others?

Successful leaders find ways to minimize that dependence. This may mean learning how to do some function that had previously been in the expertise domain of a subordinate. It may also mean becoming more skillful in dealing with dependent relationships and learning how to respond more appropriately to dependence situations. It may even mean making others more dependent upon the leader's power.

Using Power in Relationships

While Kotter's delineations of power relate to the managerial realm, there are wide applications of these concepts to virtually any interaction. It is rare that a relationship between two people or among the members of a group is based on total equity. Life is simply not that symmetrical. Ordinarily, even in peer relationships, we complement each other's needs.

Kotter asserts that having a power base increases our own effectiveness and also prevents us from being deeply hurt by others. Let us examine the types of power he has observed.[7]

Sense of obligation

Developing a sense of obligation in others as a way to increase one's own power will strike some readers as being insincere or manipulative. Remember, Kotter's research was done within the confines of corporate realities. To believe that power struggles do not occur in the business world is to demonstrate one's unfamiliarity with it.

Even in non-business situations, however, we may find the need to develop a sense of obligation. "You scratch my back and I'll scratch yours" and "One hand washes the other" are colloquial expressions which reflect this very relationship. Doing favors (which often cost very little but are genuinely appreciated) for others essentially means that we expect others to do favors for us at some point in the future.

If we view the purpose of these gestures as being the development of friendship with those we depend on, the use of power in relationships seems somehow less tainted. And yet, we do not think of these favor trade-offs among friends as being deceptive or self-aggrandizing. Why should we view favor tradeoffs among business associates as being dishonest or disreputable?

Belief in expertise

Leaders do not remain leaders very long if their followers sense the leader is a sham; that she does not know as much as she should. We expect our leaders to be superior to us, on some level at least, and we resent it when they do not conform to our expectations. One way to gain power is to establish one's reputation as an expert on some subject, for knowledge *is* power.

The class "brain" often has considerable influence over others, if not actual power, for they respect what she knows and often turn to her for assistance. The expert is listened to and is usually not contradicted by those who do not possess her specialized knowledge. The more extensive the leader's accomplishments, the more power she can exert.

In discussing this type of power, Kotter makes a valuable suggestion: be strong, even outspoken, on subjects about which you know a great deal, but remain quiet on subjects about which you know very little. His suggestion parallels the maxim, "I have never been hurt by something I did not say." Words *can* come back to haunt us, as Shakespeare noted 500 years ago when he exhorted us to mend our speech, for it has the power to mar our fortunes.

Identification

We are more likely to identify with those whom we respect, because they represent an ideal to which we aspire. By his very presence, the charismatic leader inspires us to be more than we have been. The almost magical pull such individuals have accounts for their remarkable ability to sway the opinions and actions of others. We wish to be identified with those who are widely admired for their heroism or courage or intelligence.

Is it possible to develop charismatic powers over others? Many experts believe it is. Studies of people perceived to have charisma show that such people are more animated than the average person and that they tend to make physical gestures (such as touching someone on the arm to make a point) more often than most people.

Kotter suggests we can develop charisma by displaying to our followers an idealized version of what they might become. We can dress and speak and act in ways that others admire. We can make others aware of us and our concern for them. We can give speeches about commonly shared goals or popular causes. In short, we can become a figure that others can believe in and identify with, by being worthy of their belief.

Perceived dependence

The more others believe they can depend on us to help them or prevent them from being harmed, the more power we will have over them. Kotter exhorts the power figure to actively assist her followers to obtain all possible needed resources (which may be time or money, information or influence).

The powerful manager or successful leader can and does go out of her way to secure for subordinates the things they need to do their jobs more effectively. Each time a subordinate turns to the manager for help (and receives it), the leader's power base is extended a bit more.

Creating an aura of power may mean displaying the symbols of power or associating with powerful figures. To gain power indirectly, the leader may join an organization in her field and volunteer to serve on a committee or head a task force. Professional organizations are always seeking additional help; they are usually generous in acknowledging the source of that help.

Use power to persuade and inform your subordinates; don't use it automatically and autocratically. Think of the words of General George S. Patton, a leader of considerable power: "Never tell people how to do things. Tell them what to do and they will surprise you with their ingenuity."

If you would be successful at obtaining and employing power, follow the guidelines Kotter suggests.[8]

Be sensitive

Successful power brokers understand they are expected to operate within acknowledged realms of propriety. Since power can easily be misused and even abused, the successful power-user does not operate tyrannically, nor is he a pretender to the throne of power. He repays favors, he ensures that his reputation for expertise is well-founded, he acts like an ethical leader and continually gives evidence of why people were correct to have placed their trust in him.

Understand the workings of power

The leader who would use power successfully must let intuition and experience guide him to the best use of power in various situations, with various people. Being aware of the advantages and disadvantages associated with different types of power, he judiciously selects the most appropriate type. He persuades when persuasion works best and influences with power when that strategy works best.

Develop all your power skills

Managers who excel at influencing others have taken pains to extend their power skills. They will use obligation, expertise, identification or perceived dependence as necessary. At other times they will seek to persuade. They do, in short, what must be done to achieve organizational aims without compromising propriety or ethics.

Seek positions to match your power skills

To maximize the use of power, the manager/leader pursues career goals compatible with his ability to use power. Individuals uncomfortable with being perceived as an expert in a given area (either because they are shy or do not like to be in the limelight or because they do not believe their expertise is unusual) will have difficulty exerting expert power. And not to develop any one kind of power lessens the leader's overall effectiveness.

Use your power strategically

Kotter proposes that managers view their power as capital which can be parlayed into even more power. Granted, the jockeying for power positions doesn't always work. Sometimes the power player has less return on his power investment than she started with, but such risks are part of all human transactions. The knowledgeable power-user views each situation carefully and then deploys her power wisely, giving up power in one situation in order to obtain even more power in a different situation.

Use power in moderation

Temperance is employed by the most accomplished users of power. As we mentioned before, power should not be used all of the time, in all relationships, in all circumstances. Nor should it be used for self-serving purposes.

Become comfortable with power

The leader who uses power well is aware of the good uses to which it can be put; she has accepted the ramifications of using power, knowing it is necessary if she is to operate in the most efficient manner. Power is just one more vehicle to facilitate accomplishment.

Most people do not think about their potential for power. The leader does. She is willing to use her power over others to make things happen. She extends her influence whenever she can, with whatever tools she has or can borrow.

Summary

As we explore leadership traits and leadership styles, we will find that leadership is demonstrated by words or by actions; the actions themselves usually have words associated with them. Through her words and through her actions, we come to believe we can trust our leader. She is predictable, in a sense, for she says and does what we ex·pect her to say and do. We choose to place our faith in her because we believe she can affect the course of our lives.

The leader has the ability to conceive of a goal and to achieve that goal through positive interactions with others—interactions that depend upon words as the medium of expression.

Whether the leader is employing an autocratic style of leadership, a democratic style or a laissez-faire style, the leader is communicating that style via her words. When the leader selects the situational style of leadership, she knows that different verbal styles are suitable for different situations, individuals, and power exchanges.

Power, according to John Kotter, does not mean self-interest or Machiavellian tactics. The same is true for the language of power: it must be used to make things happen, to coalesce people and purpose for the ultimate good of the organization. Kotter reviews for us how successful managers influence others—either by persuasion or by power. The leader eager to serve as catalyst while participating in the catalytic process knows he must use the four different types of power: sense of obligation, belief in expertise, identification, perceived dependence—all of which are made apparent to others via the communication process.

In the following chapter, we shall take a closer look at how power impacts language as we study one specific aspect of the language of leadership, namely, the language of power.

Answers (pages 18 and 19)

1. Haste makes waste.
2. Don't look a gift horse in the mouth.
3. Don't cut off your nose to spite your face.
4. Don't cross the bridge until you come to it.
5. Don't put all your eggs in one basket.
6. Brevity is the soul of wit.
7. Love makes the world go round.
8. A picture is worth a thousand words.
9. Absence makes the heart grow fonder.

1.	G	11.	F
2.	L	12.	E
3.	Q	13.	D
4.	M	14.	A
5.	J	15.	I
6.	C	16.	S
7.	R	17.	P
8.	H	18.	T
9.	N	19.	K
10.	B	20.	O

Footnotes

[1] Lee Iacocca and William Novak, *Iacocca: An Autobiography* (New York, Bantam Books, 1984), pp. 58–59. Reprinted with permission.

[2] From the *Quarterly Review of Doublespeak,* Copyright © National Council of Teachers of English. Reprinted with permission.

[3] Lee Iacocca and William Novak, *Iacocca: An Autobiography* (New York, Bantam Books, 1984), p. 55. Reprinted with permission.

[4] Reprinted by permission of the *Harvard Business Review.* Excerpt from "Power, Dependence and Effective Management" by John P. Kotter (July-August 1977). Copyright © 1977 by the President and Fellows of Harvard College; all rights reserved.

[5] Ibid.

[6] Ibid.

[7] Ibid.

[8] Ibid.

CHAPTER TWO:
The Language of Power:
A Study of Lee Iacocca's Words

> *Above all, he gave the world for an imperishable moment the vision of a leader who greatly understood the terror and the hope, the diversity and the possibility, of life on this planet and who made people look beyond nation and race to the future of humanity.*
>
> Arthur M. Schlesinger, Jr.
> writing about John F. Kennedy

Introduction

Each of us is called upon from time to time to demonstrate leadership. No matter what the occasion, there are certain common behaviors exhibited when leaders take charge of a situation by taking charge of others. While leadership involves a great many traits, none is more important than the ability to communicate well, to share the vision of which Schlesinger speaks.

Twenty years ago, Harvard University conducted a study and found that of all the criteria by which leadership and/or promotional potential is assessed, the most significant trait, according to the executives interviewed, was the ability to communicate well.

More recently a *Fortune 500* survey of top executives revealed that the quality considered most important for promotion to a position of leadership was not technical excellence, not financial knowledge, not marketing ability, but communication skill.

What is communicated by those leaders, by those men and women to whom we so willingly pledge allegiance, beside whom we want to stand be counted? What is it about leaders' language that excites us and inspires us to be more than we have been? How do leaders help us become aware of "the diversity and the possibility," to which Schlesinger alludes?

Leaders, above all else, motivate us. They find the essence of our worth and then they call upon that recognized merit. We find ourselves wanting to follow, to be told what to do. Leaders share their vision with us —they invite us to participate in the realization of a goal.

We are inspired, of course, because of the leader's behavior. Upon that behavior, we can mold our own. More often, though, we are inspired by her words. The leader's understanding of power, of politics, of persuasion and of psychology is evident in her expression. The leader knows the power of words and their likely effect upon an audience. She depends on an understanding of, and facility with, the powerful, political, persuasive, and psychological underpinnings of effective communication.

Language that moves us to action is not a haphazard occurrence: it is carefully planned to employ those elements mentioned above, in order to maximize results. We shall examine the words of various leaders in an effort to better comprehend how leadership language affects power, politics, persuasion and psychology.

Practice: Think of someone you regard as a leader. What special leadership language elements does this person depend on? Which of those elements could you incorporate into your own style?

Theory of Acquired Needs

As we go through life to become what we are, we acquire needs along the way. According to David McClelland, who has studied people in corporations for over 30 years, each of us is motivated by different needs. If these acquired needs can be matched to jobs, he postulates, greater success and satisfaction will follow. The broad need categories that McClelland has delineated are the following:

Need for achievement
Individuals driven by this need often enjoy working alone on projects that intrigue them. They enjoy figuring out ways to improve the efficiency of people, systems, and mechanisms. Good problem-sol-

vers, achievement-oriented individuals like challenges, like concentrating on difficult tasks, like the satisfaction that comes from knowing a job has been well-done. While they do not necessarily dislike working with other people, they usually prefer setting their own goals and accomplishing them alone. They work in isolation fairly easily. Examples of persons with high achievement needs might be engineers, writers, artists, lawyers or salespeople with their own territory.

Need for affiliation

People who are driven by the need for affiliation usually wind up in service-oriented jobs. They become social workers or customer-service representatives or waitresses, for example, They select positions that allow them to interact with others, rather than work in virtual isolation at a desk or computer terminal. Often, such persons do volunteer work, for they enjoy—sometimes even require—the satisfaction that results from having assisted others.

Need for power

It is important to remember that power itself is not necessarily a corrupting influence. It is only when power is abused that negative consequences occur. Ideally, individuals who enjoy being in command, being recognized for what their unit or group has accomplished, will use power for the good of the organization. Those whose primary acquired need is the need for power often become military leaders or executives.

It is the power aspect of leadership that we will consider first. Whether you are chairing a meeting, serving as the captain of your bowling team, organizing a fund-raiser or motivating your subordinates to increase productivity, you must exert some control over those individuals. People comfortable with power are most successful when they evince ethical responsibility toward organizational goals, rather than toward personal ambitions. If you have not yet acquired confidence and comfort in using power, and if you are eager to develop your leadership skills, commit to learning more about the various types of power.

Practice: The research indicates that the most successful executives are those who have a strong power drive. Why do you think this is so?

Do a self-assessment and pinpoint the need which most motivates you.

Types of Power

In the preceding chapter, we cited the two types of power Kotter identifies: position power and persuasion power. There are other types of power as well, each of them having linguistic attributes of their own. Here are fuller definitions and examples of the various kinds of power.

Legitimate power

Legitimate power (often called "position power") is the power that rightfully accrues to a person primarily because of *what*, not who, he is. By virtue of being in a position of leadership, the president of a fraternity and the Chief Executive Officer (CEO) of a manufacturing firm both share the same kind of power enjoyed by the President of the United States: the power legitimately associated with that position.

This type of power is the embodiment of authority; it carries the clout given to the position-holder by the formal structure of the organization. By not recognizing or by not using legitimate power, the position-holder will soon erode the legitimate power that others are willing to accord him by virtue of his stature.

Coercive power

Coercive power is used by individuals who have the power to punish or reward others. As children, we yielded to parents who had the power to reprimand, or to offer positive consequences for good behavior. We, as a rule, did what they wanted us to do, because they maintained control over us through coercive power. As students, we again had our behaviors shaped, in part, by the ability of teachers and professors to punish or reward us with grades. And when we entered the working world, we found superiors using coercive power as a natural extension of the legitimate power associated with their roles.

The use of coercive power, of course, goes beyond the classroom or the workplace. It often infiltrates our personal relationships as well. As we use coercive power on others, so others use coercive power on us. Think about the number of relationships you experience in a given week in which coercive power is used—by you or by the other person. The number is probably higher than you initially thought it would be.

Expert power

Expert power is employed by those whose specialized skills and knowledge enable them to have some control over others who do not have the same expertise or information. Knowledge *is* power, as we have noted before, and those who seem to "have all the answers" enjoy the limelight they are put in when others turn to them (and often only them) for assistance.

Akin to expert power is the power derived from having information. Within any organization are those who work hard to obtain information (and sometimes gossip) and use it to their own advantage. They dole it out to selected recipients and thereby enjoy their role as keeper-of-the-latest-organizational-news.

Charismatic power

Charismatic power is in effect when individuals who wish to be aligned with an attractive person offer their allegiance to that person. The leader who is attractive, literally attractive, by virtue of a charismatic personality often finds that she can exert some control over others seeking to identify with someone who is perceived to be outstanding in one way or another.

Charismatic power goes beyond popularity; charismatic individuals somehow draw others into their presence. They exert a power over others without even trying to, it seems. There are those followers of charismatic leaders who give willingly of their time, money and effort. For example, volunteer campaign aides of a charismatic political leader will often make personal sacrifices for a leader whom they support.

Practice: As mentioned earlier, charismatic leaders are more animated than the average person. In addition, they tend to smile more, enunciate better, talk more rapidly and move their arms and heads more frequently. Rate yourself on a scale of one to ten (or, have others rate you) in terms of these specific charismatic traits.

Association power

Association power can be obtained by associating in some way with powerful individuals. Such power is a secondary power, as it is derived, not from any inherent superiority, but from influence achieved only because of some connection with a truly powerful figure.

For example, if the wife of the base commander is employed as a typist in the typing pool, she will enjoy association power by virtue of her marriage, regardless of any special talents she herself may or may not possess. This peripheral power is obviously not as deep as other types of power, but it can be used, nonetheless, to the advantage of its holder.

These are the types of power most often recognized, but there are other types of power as well. For example, situational power imbues individuals in relatively unimportant positions with a temporary power over us—power specific to a particular incident or situation.

Take for example the ticket agent who is processing your ticket for a flight leaving in five minutes. She has the power to speed up the paperwork to help you make your flight. But if she is unwilling to find shortcuts or work a little faster, she will cause you to miss the flight. For those few short moments of your life, you are dependent upon the person who has situational power over you.

Practice: Think about a situation in which someone exerted this type of power over you. Describe your reaction.

Speaking of dependency brings us to another kind of power. Paradoxically, the individuals who are dependent upon us sometimes exert a power over us. That power may be operant guilt, which forces us to continue supporting or protecting or providing for those whom we know depend on us. But dependency power, with all its psychological ramifications, is usually not evident in healthy relationships.

Leadership is synonymous with power. To become an influential leader, you must become comfortable with power. It is important, therefore, for you to examine how you feel about the various kinds of power and the uses to which they are put—by you and by others in your environment.

Practice: What are some other types of power? Describe them.

THE ASPECTS OF LEADERSHIP LANGUAGE

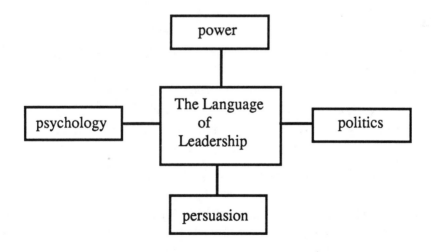

The Language of Power

The words of the individual who has been termed "the most famous and most popular American businessman" by *Fortune* magazine will be the primary focus of our consideration of the language of power and the correlative power of language. Lido Anthony Iacocca is the leader upon whom Warren Bennis and Burt Nanus have based their book *Leaders: The Strategies for Taking Charge*.

Almost exclusively because of Iacocca's leadership, by 1983 Chrysler made a profit, boosted employee morale, and helped employees generate a sense of meaning in their work. He empowered them. In fact, we believe that Iacocca's high visibility symbolizes the missing element in management today (and much of management theory) in that his style of leadership is central to organizational success. Our concept of power and leadership, then, is modeled on the Iacocca phenomenon: power is the basic energy needed to initiate and sustain action, or to put it another way, the *capacity to translate intention into reality and sustain it*. Leadership is the wise use of this power: *Transformative* leadership.[9]

Empowering

True leaders have so much power they are willing to give it away. Power is not a fixed, quantifiable sum; instead it is an unlimited abstraction which grows as it is shared. We find this sense of empowerment as a recurrent pattern in a commencement address which Iacocca recently delivered at the University of Southern California (USC). We also find an honest self-assessment, an employment of language that is powerful— direct and straightforward and stripped of illusions:

"Dr. Zumberge was very kind in his introduction, and I appreciate it very much. He said I left Ford after 32 years to take on a big challenge at Chrysler. And, by the way, he was nice enough to leave out a few of the details. Actually, what happened was I got fired. And I went to Chrysler because the auto industry happened to be my life, and because Chrysler was the only game in town at that moment...with an open seat.

"I was not looking for a challenge, and neither were the thousands of men and women who surprised the world by bringing Chrysler back from the dead. We were all just trying to survive, that's all. No more—no less.

"Chrysler Corporation is alive today not because those men and women went looking for a challenge (they would have had to be crazy to do that), but because they had the moxie to accept a challenge that all the so-called experts from Wall Street to Washington told them was hopeless.

"You see, the easiest challenges are the ones you dream up for yourself; the tough ones (the really lousy ones) are those that just get dropped in your lap."

We see, in this leader at least, a willingness to deal with the unvarnished truth, to strip away those verbal embellishments which soften truth's severity. Iacocca's admission of what really happened is a refreshing change. We have become used to the nuances of color which strategically placed words can give to a black-and-white issue. Iacocca "tells it like it is," to coin the vernacular.

He speaks in bold, black-and-white phrases and does not hesitate to reject the experts' advice and accept his own instead.

More than two decades ago, Robert Townsend observed, "Something is happening to our country. We aren't producing leaders like we used to. A new chief executive officer today, exhausted by the climb to the peak, falls down on the mountain and goes to sleep."

Honest

That same metaphorical mountain is identified by Iacocca twice. First, at the beginning of his address, as he critically assesses the legacy left by one generation to another:

"But here's my first piece of advice for you today: Don't go looking for new mountains to climb until you get to the top of the one you're on.

"And the one you're on right now—the slope on which my generation has left your generation—is steep, and it's strenuous, and (I hate to tell you) a little slippery.

"You're coming of age in a country that has begun to ask itself an awful, awful question and one that it has never asked itself before—and I mean never! And the question is simple: 'Can we compete?' Competitiveness has become the big buzz word all over the country now. Especially in Washington, D.C. (where, by the way, they don't really understand it). The question is: Can we keep going up that mountain that Americans have been climbing for 100 years? Or have we reached the limit of our endurance? And will yours be the first generation not to go higher?"

Second, near the end of his address, he again answers those questions in a most positive way. He asserts the need for leadership if the mountaintop is to be reached:

"You are a long way from the top of that mountain I mentioned a couple of minutes ago. In fact, the top isn't even in sight. The end of the American Century doesn't mean the decline of America. It simply means that millions of people around the world have looked at what we have here, and said, 'Hey, we'd like a little of that, too.'

"That's part of the legacy of the American Century. We can all be proud that the tide of human expectations throughout the world is rising because of our example, but it doesn't mean that it has to rise at our expense, does it? You can go farther up that mountain, but only if you use your leadership."

Inspiring

The supporting words which lead to inspiration and ultimately to empowerment are repeated at the very end of his remarks. The can-do spirit, the defiance, the refusal to accept defeat must have made the audience feel that the world truly was their oyster, with pearls to be had just for the trying.

"Don't believe all those who say that your generation will be the first generation of Americans that will have to settle for less. I don't believe that for a minute so don't you believe it. When anybody says that to you, just tell them to get the hell out of your way!"

The conclusion refers to the metaphor once again, personalizes the event (via the USC reference) and inspires the listeners to maximize their potential. The words are the words of a coach or of a parent.

"And finally, don't let anybody tell you that you can't keep going up that mountain because with the brains you got from God and a little help from USC—you'll do just fine."

We can believe the leader who is wise enough to admit that he doesn't have (nor does anyone else) all the answers, confident enough to empower others with finding at least some of the answers. Note here the use of humor, of familiar references ("final exams"), and of reassurance.

"Relax, but don't go to sleep, because tomorrow the real final exams start. And they'll go on for the rest of your lives. I'm going to give a little peek at the exam, but I won't be able to help you with the answers. They are going to have to come from you.

"Let me warn you, there are no road maps. Unfortunately, I can't leave you a road map today. You see, I don't know what kind of leadership it's going to take for America to compete in the 21st Century. You are going to have to figure that out all by yourselves. You'll have to take a look at the problems, and you'll have to come up with your own solutions. And don't be scared—every generation has had to do that."

Critically assessing

In a further demonstration of honest, perhaps painful, scrutiny, we find Iacocca doing what leaders must do; upholding the tenets of the "emperor-has-no-clothes"-ism. Probing beneath the glitter (as Governor Mario Cuomo also does in the next section), Iacocca delivers some harsh realities. He critically assesses a situation and then shares that assessment, even though his words may not be welcomed.

He tells the graduates:

"When you came in as freshmen, the United States was the largest creditor nation in the world. American banks were the largest in the world, and Wall Street was the undisputed center of the financial universe.

"As you graduate today, our country is the world's largest debtor (with more debt spread around the globe than Mexico and Brazil combined); four of the five largest banks in the world today are in Japan, and so...is the world's largest stock exchange.

"When you were freshmen, America was still the breadbasket of the world, but today as you leave, more farmers are losing their land than at any time since the dust bowl days of the Great Depression.

"And I'm sure you must have been told as freshmen that America's world leadership in science and high-tech was insurmountable, and that it virtually guaranteed your future prosperity. Well, now we've got a trade deficit in high tech. And we've just slapped some tough tariffs on the Japanese to try to deny them a worldwide monopoly in the most crucial technology of the day."

Practice: Critically assess some situation facing America today and then write a brief statement about it reflecting your honest opinions and inspiring the reader at the same time.

Hardworking

The leader recognizes that hard work is synonymous with success. He is bold enough to tell his followers that he has expectations of them.

"I think it [the theme of a fund-raising program] captures what this university has tried to give you, and also what it expects from you. That theme, of course, is 'Leadership for the 21st Century.'

"It's going to take a different kind of leadership to shoulder all this debt and keep moving up that mountain, because the 21st Century is going to be different for America."

Detail-oriented

The leader, having taken the trouble to obtain facts to substantiate his points—chilling points in this case—deliberately seeks to reach his audience, to motivate them, to make them uncomfortable enough to go out and make changes in the world. He uses specific details to further emphasize those points.

"So, a lot's been happening while you've been in school. But, you might say, 'Hey, wait a minute!' Things don't *look* all that bad, do they? Maybe you don't know it, but you are one of those rare classes that have gone all the way through school from your first day as freshmen to today, without even a hint of a recession—that's 17 straight quarters of economic growth! The stock market has gone up since you arrived on campus that first day—it's gone up 1,000 points while you've been here. It went from 1300 to 2400 in the Dow Jones. Income is way up in those four years. Taxes are way down. These have really been the 'Feel Good Times,' right?"

Practice: Use details to substantiate an expectation you have for others. They may be colleagues, subordinates, family members, group members, etc. Try to paint so realistic a picture that they will feel compelled to bring about change in their current practices.

Myth-shattering

The leader is a myth-shatterer. He brings reality to his audience. He pricks the grandiose balloons of superficial appearance with pins of truth. Listen as Iacocca tells us the "Feel-Good Times" were not.

"Well, that's what we thought. But we've suddenly sobered up to find that our trip through the 'feel-good' eighties has been chemically induced by a dope called debt. And I hate to be the one to bring you the bad news, but we've run up that debt on our credit cards.

"While you've had your noses in the books, we've quietly been doubling the national debt. It took us two centuries to book our first trillion dollars of debt, and by the way, that included eight wars, a couple of depressions, the opening of the West, the Square Deal, the Fair Deal, the New Deal, the Great Society, and the terms of 39 Presidents."

Motivating

The language of leadership is calculated to move the listener or the reader to action. Here, the audience is encouraged, even prodded, to right a wrong:

"But while you weren't looking, we just made it two trillion—and we did that in just a little over five years—and those were five years of peace and prosperity.

Now, if I'm starting to stir you a little or even make you mad—that's good. That's what I'm supposed to do here today."

Emotional

The leader is not hesitant to share his emotions:

"Because I am not proud of the kind of debt we're handing you. In fact, I'm truly embarrassed by it. Nobody stuck me with a due-bill like this when I was your age. And nobody wondered out loud back then whether America could compete, because we had taught the whole world what competing was all about in the first place. I sat in your place in those happy days at the end of World War II when America was flush with victory, and we were the new leaders of the whole world.

"Believe it or not, back in those innocent days, a lot of people really thought we had a chance to build a perfect world, but a few things went wrong. There were a couple more wars, there were eight recessions, there was Watergate, and a dozen other man-made disasters along the way."

Nor is the leader hesitant to provoke the emotions of his audience. In the following excerpt, Iacocca uses (as does Cuomo in the next chapter) a metaphorical image to contrast real wealth and the facade of wealth.

"To be honest with you, we're handing you more than anybody has ever passed on to their kids. Generations ahead of you were lucky if they inherited a little shack on the back forty. You're getting a big, beautiful mansion on a hill. That's what we're leaving you.

"But, just one thing before you get all choked up with gratitude: we haven't bothered to pay for all this yet. We're leaving you the mansion, all right, but it's got a little mortgage on it.

"You've got a right to be mad about that mortgage, and if you're as smart as your degrees say you are, you're going to do something about it."

Practice: Shatter a myth as Iacocca did. As you prepare this communication about a myth in your environment, try to motivate your audience. Do not hesitate to appeal to their emotions or to reveal your own.

Confident

In that last quoted sentence above, we hear expressed again the confidence the leader has in the ability of followers to do something important, to make a difference in their own world. The leader helps his followers to believe in themselves. He does this, in part, by creating an enthusiasm for a challenging project:

"I hope you're all leaving here today with a certain sense of adventure. I hope you're all itching, in fact, to climb a couple of mountains."

Proud

Almost inevitably, the leader expresses pride in her accomplishments and in the accomplishment of her associates. Such pride is evident in Iacocca's words as well:

"...we did manage to wipe out a few diseases. We put a man on the moon. We produced more technological change than all of those who came before us, and I mean combined."

Ethical

We also learn that the leader, as personified by Lee Iacocca, considers the ethics of behavior:

"And we made America, I think, a little bit more just, a little more fair, and maybe, just maybe, a little bit more humane."

The sense of fair play can be found throughout his address:

"Today, the importance of the American market gives us all the muscle we need to forge a trading system that's fair to us and fair to our friends around the world. And it's that market that still makes us leaders in world trade—at least for a while longer."

Responsible

The leader recognizes that leadership entails more than just strength: it also entails a sense of duty. As Iacocca asserts, being a leader means being responsible.

"It's not going to be the 'American Century' again, for one thing. We're not going to dominate the 21st Century like we have the 20th. Hopefully, nobody will, by the way—it's better that way. We're going to have to compete for most of what we now take for granted, including our standard of living. And it takes stronger and wiser leadership to compete than it does to dominate."

Returning to an earlier comment about chosen challenges and those which are thrust upon us, Iacocca provides a historical challenge about America's leadership position:

"Our domination and our leadership came by default, when you think about it—not because we sought it. We happened to be there to pick up the pieces after World War II, but no nation (and remember this) has ever exercised its domination more generously, or its leadership more responsibly, than we have. That's the legacy of the American Century that we are going to leave to history, and it's a proud one.

"I'm not bothered for a minute by the thought that America may not dominate the 21st Century, but it scares the hell out of me to think that we might also give up our leadership."

Practice: Prepare a message for others that contains the following elements: enthusiasm, pride, confidence. That statement should also reflect an ethical, responsible stance.

Future-oriented

Walter Lippman opines that "the final test of a leader is that he leaves behind him in other men the conviction and the will to carry on." Through his challenge, his encouragement, and his warning, Iacocca passes the torch and the will to future leaders.

"But that proud legacy may also turn out to be our epitaph if we don't learn to compete effectively in the world that we have so generously and so responsibly helped to create.

"And today, we are not competing effectively. The red ink is up to our knees, and still rising. Of our 20 largest trading partners, we're in deficit with 17 of them, now. Oh, we have small surpluses (very small) with Holland, and Belgium and Australia, but after those countries, we have to rely on such lush and lucrative markets as Paraguay, Greenland and the Falkland Islands! We even had surpluses with Russia, Vietnam and Libya, believe it or not. But we've had trouble selling much of anything to our friends."

Firm

But leaders are able to see possibilities where others just see problems. John F. Kennedy spoke of our needing "a new generation of leadership, to cope with new problems and new opportunities. For there is a new world to be won." Similarly, Iacocca speaks of the need for leaders to recognize the real cause of problems so that the right solutions can be found. His position is a strong one.

> "We can blame our friends overseas who have repaid our generosity with policies calculated to enrich themselves at our expense. We can blame them for flooding our open market while they shut us out of theirs.
>
> "But we certainly have to blame ourselves for this blind consumption binge that we've been on.
>
> "And we have to blame ourselves for worshipping so long at the altar of 'free trade' that we've become blind to how the world really works out there. We've got this silly notion that it's a mortal sin to play by the rules everybody else is using— even to protect ourselves."

Realistic

In a graphic comparison, Iacocca likens vulnerable American businesses to "those few crazy hockey players who still refuse to wear helmets," and who, as a result, are having their "brains beat out." But he recognizes the necessity of moving past blame: "So there's lots of blame out there, but it's not the job of leaders to find blame: it's the job of leaders to lead!"

His words echo a sentiment expressed many years earlier by Harry Truman: "A leader has to lead, or otherwise he has no business in politics." But Iacocca identifies other responsibilities the leader must bear:

> "It's the job of leaders to set the rules and to enforce the rules, and most important, when the rules don't work any more, to change the rules."

Definitive

In a series of equally strong, definitive statements, Iacocca continues to explain what leaders are and what they are not:

"I know for sure that we'll give it [leadership] up if we don't get rid of this brutal debt load that we're carrying as a nation. Debtors aren't leaders. It's the guy holding the IOU's who calls the shots. But, our record of borrow and spend, borrow and spend—with the bills passed on to you, our kids—that's not the kind of record that makes you a world leader."

Practice: Think about a future eventuality. Then prepare a brief essay in which you suggest ways for the reader to deal with that possibility. Be realistic, firm, and definite. Don't be tempted to lay blame on others but instead pinpoint what the present generation has done to pave the way for that likely condition of the future.

Opinionated

Unafraid to take a strong stand on an issue about which he has unshakable feelings, Iacocca cautions:

"We're already seeing some of the dangers of that debt burden in the current trade debate, by the way. We're being warned now (literally warned) that we can't defend ourselves against some clearly unfair practices of our trading partners, because if we do, those countries will cut off the financing that we've become hooked on to cover the debt."

This concern about being a debtor nation—"So we're becoming hostages to our own debt, and it doesn't take a degree from USC to figure out that hostages can't be leaders, either."—appears often in Iacocca's commentary. For example, in remarks he made to the National Governors' Association on July 25, 1987, Iacocca gave (in view of the subsequent Japanese purchase of Rockefeller Square) a prescient warning:

"Let me tell you what we're up against as a nation right now. This is a quote from Wataru Hiraizumi, a prominent member of the Japanese Diet, talking to an American reporter:

Quote. 'Japan is not going to change. We love to work hard and Americans don't.... The result is that we'll continue to work hard and amass huge surpluses of money. We'll buy up your land and you'll live there and pay rent. We won't go to war. We won't destroy each other. We're condemned to live together.'"

Competitive

But the fighting spirit resurges, in both the Governors' Association Speech—"Mr. Hiraizumi has a lot to learn about Americans if he thinks that scenario will ever play out"—and in the commencement address.

"But we don't have to let ourselves be held hostage—to anybody—because even though the rest of the world can get along (and they can) without our steel, and our cars, and our grain, and even our high-tech now, we've got a hole card that tops anything the others can lay out on the table.

"And it's called the American market. (That's our ace of spades; don't forget it.)"

The firm position is evident in his historical assessment of the current trade situation:

"But for years now, the Japanese have taken one hundred percent of their total worldwide automotive profits from just one, single market—ours!

"We haven't had the same access to foreign markets, of course. We didn't even ask for it for a long time because we wanted to give our friends a chance to develop. But when they were up and running (and in many ways, were even more competitive than we were), we asked very politely for equal treatment and their doors still stayed closed.

"We should have pushed those doors open, but we didn't. That was also a failure of leadership, by the way, because leaders don't let themselves get pushed around."

Cognizant of the power the weak can hold over the strong, Iacocca advises his audience against permitting others to become too dependent:

"By not having the leadership to insist on fair and equal treatment, we've encouraged our friends to become overdependent on the American market. And I might add, in the process, we've shipped millions of American jobs overseas, and buried ourselves under a dungheap of public debt.

"But our friends overseas can't afford it, either. Remember, you never do anybody a favor in the long run by letting them become too dependent on you."

The topic of fairness emerges again as Iacocca expounds on the trade imbalance (a situation that disturbs a number of other American business leaders, such as Donald Trump).

"So, we're unfair to ourselves, and we're unfair to them [friends overseas] by allowing the United States to become the world's shopping mall—a giant bazaar where everybody comes to pitch a tent and peddle their wares—and there are no questions ever asked!

"It's really time to start charging admission to the American market...and the price of a ticket has to be a little fairness, and a little reciprocity. If we're leaders, then it's our responsibility to set some rules, for a change."

Practice: What issue do you have definite opinions about? Discuss that issue and let a competitive, fighting spirit come through as you present your point of view.

Encouraging

Power figures such as Lee Iacocca do not fail to consider the ramifications of current practices upon future eventualities:

"But with leadership, you either use it, or lose it. That's the great danger that America faces in our trade relations today, and that's the great danger we all face in the years ahead."

and to recommend how solutions can be found for those anticipated problems. The address concludes with a challenge: we hear the leader manifest his faith in those who will carry on after him; we hear him empower them through his belief in their strength. He exhorts them to succeed:

"There's nothing, absolutely nothing in it [the Constitution] that will tell you what kind of leaders to be for the 21st Century. There's nothing in it to tell you how to protect the environment or what to do about terrorists or how to reduce the threat of nuclear war or how to compete in the world. Nothing.

"The Founding Fathers were too smart to tell you (or me)— 200 years later—how to solve your problems. You see, they left us a little framework to protect our freedom, but they didn't tell you anything about how to use it.

"So, I'm sorry, but I'm not going to tell you how to use it either, but I will leave you with a few hints on how not to use it. This is the lesson:

- Don't look for all the answers neatly tucked away in one ideology or another, because you're never going to find them.

- Don't let the people with the pat answers ever take over. The extremists (from either direction) will always screw things up if you put them in charge.

- Don't be afraid to compromise when you can't win, and don't be afraid to dig in your heels and fight like hell when you think you can.

- Don't be so idealistic that you can't see what's going on in the world around you, but don't be so pragmatic that you don't ever stand for anything.

- Don't be afraid to make mistakes, but for starters try to practice with the small ones, okay? And, oh, don't make the same big mistake twice.

The leadership traits that we see so admirably exemplified in Mr. Iacocca's speech are depicted in this diagram.

COMPONENTS OF THE LANGUAGE OF POWER

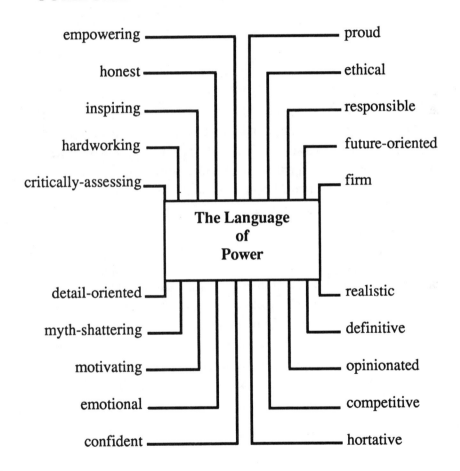

Upon Iacocca's recommendation, we will practice with small language mistakes, in the hope of avoiding the big mistakes. In time, perhaps we may lay claim to the mastery that he himself demonstrates in his language of leadership.

As we have noted, language is the primary vehicle by which we express the control we have over others, control that is needed if we are to exert any real influence, if we are to make any real difference in the lives of those who follow us. To make an impact in our work milieu, we must be able to inspire or encourage others to work cooperatively so the aims of the organization can be accomplished. In the examples that follow, we will examine some real-world communications in which language actually undermines the leader's power.

Situation:

Upper management of your firm has decided that your job has become so expanded that you should have an assistant. The assistant will report directly to you. The three managers who used to report to you will now report to your assistant. While each of the three managers has officially applied for the newly created position, you have chosen to hire from outside the firm. You have decided to inform the managers of your decision with an inter-office memo. Here is the first draft of your memo.

Sample:

Although each of you is eminently qualified to assume the role of my assistant, I have decided to select a person for that role who comes to us from another company. As of Monday, June 15, Mr. Henry Johnson will be the new assistant to the director. It is expected that each of you will report directly to him on all operational matters. I hope you will do all you can to work cooperatively with Mr. Johnson and to help acclimate him to our firm.

Analysis:

This memo, albeit professional in its tone and syntax, fails to reinforce the leader's power. What flaws did you note as you read the communication?

As the three managers read this memo, they were probably offended by the reference to their eminent qualifications. First of all, it is unlikely that they are equally qualified and to suggest so is to insult the superior manager and to make the less-qualified doubt the leader's sincerity.

By mentioning their qualifications, the writer is rubbing metaphoric salt into a wound. Not only were they *not* chosen, but they are reminded that they were sufficiently qualified to have *been* chosen. If they are "eminently qualified" and didn't get the job, then Mr. Johnson must be extraordinarily eminently qualified to have been selected. This aura of assumed excellence may make it difficult for him to prove his competence. And, the managers will no doubt ask themselves why their eminent qualifications were not sufficient to afford them this advancement.

Finally, this brief memo fails to assert that the writer will no longer be their direct link to upper management. "It is expected" and "on all operational matters" imply they may still turn to her, if they wish, for non-operational matters that might arise. The "I hope" phrase suggests that she is dependent upon her subordinates' cooperation, that she is making a request rather than issuing a directive. Further, to imply that Mr. Johnson may need help acclimating to his new environment further reduces his chances for early success.

The explication of this brief memo examines only what was written. It is also weak because of items that were *not* written. The memo could have been strengthened by the inclusion of additional information about Mr. Johnson. The managers would probably have been somewhat mollified if they had learned that Mr. Johnson, for example, "brings 20 years' experience to the position." Such information about his outstanding background might have helped the manager-applicants to understand why they had not been chosen.

A further consideration of the communication process might have led the writer to tell her subordinates informally about the hiring decision and then follow up that information in a formal written communication.

Remember that the language of power includes the use of "power" words. Often these words come from the sports, military or financial realms. Power-people avoid "soft" words; they have learned to expunge the "I'm sorry" phrase from their expression. They tend to use imperative sentences (starting with a strong verb) rather than expletives ("It is expected....").

Practice: Here are words associated with the game of tennis: *backhand, backspin, chop, dead ball, double fault, seeding, smash, match point, take the net, trajectory.*

Select another sport in which you may be interested and compile a list of words connected to that field. Then make a conscious effort to use some of those words, if only in your spoken communications.

Imagine the following scenario; then study this draft of a letter you might have written in response to that scenario. Would this choice of words vitiate or strengthen the managerial power of the writer?

Situation:

The company president, long recognized for his community service, has asked you to distribute a memo to all employees asking for their time as volunteers in the Adopt-a-School program, which brings schools and business together. Since you believe this is a worthwhile project, you hope to enlist a number of volunteers to participate in the numerous activities.

Sample:

1) I would like to inform you about a wonderful program which tells teenagers about the world of work. 2) I know you will be dying to volunteer your time once you know more about what this program does. 3) I would like to tell you, without further ado, about this program. 4) In an effort to introduce young people to the opportunities available to them in a fantastic company such as ours, we would like to have employees donate as many hours as they can to speak at high

school assemblies about the training required for entry-level positions. 5) Additionally, we would love to have volunteers to take the young people on tours. 6) I know you will want to sign up right away, so see Gilda for further details.

Analysis:

It is clear that the adjectives selected ("wonderful," fantastic") are not power adjectives and therefore inappropriate in a professional setting calling for leadership language. The choice of verbs is equally powerless: "dying to" and "love to."

The memo fails on a number of other levels as well. Syntactically, virtually every sentence has a subject-verb-direct object order. Four of the six sentences begin with the same word: "I." While there is nothing wrong with this kind of repetition, it fails to make the writing interesting.

We need variety in our sentence structure as much as we need it in our daily lives. Surely, we would object to having the same dinner six nights in a row or wearing the same shirt (even if it were freshly laundered) six days in a row. Similarly, the effective communicator realizes she must bring variety to her sentence structure.

The second and sixth sentences begin with an assumption which may cause some readers to take umbrage: "I know you will be dying to volunteer your time...." "I know you will want to sign up right away...." And the request for employees to donate time should be placed later in the memo, so the reader will have an opportunity to learn more about the program and therefore be more inclined to participate in it.

The fourth sentence could deter potential volunteers with the phrase "as many hours as you can." If you, as the author, had considered psychological motivations, you might have realized that most employees would be willing to say "yes" *after* they had learned about the worth of the request than before they know what the request involves.

Also, you should have realized that people are more willing to contribute time or money if they feel their contribution need not involve large amounts. Once they become interested, their contributions often do increase, but stating the request from the outset may cause discomfort or stress for readers who feel they cannot afford to give much time or money.

There is no evidence of the "you" emphasis. The writer does not appeal to the benefits the reader can derive by participating. Try to present *your* requests in terms of how the reader can profit.

This writer also failed to use reference power. If you had written this memo, you should have begun by saying that the request was coming from the company president. Probably, you would have had more employees willing to consider, if not actually join, the program.

Another problem in this brief communication is its failure to realize how many people would be reluctant to speak in front of an assembly of 1,000 high school students. If the reader had not already decided to avoid this request, the fourth sentence alone would undoubtedly convince him to keep his charity at home.

The overall organization of the memo seems disjointed; that impression is deepened in Sentence 6 with the suggestion to see Gilda for further information. If the reader has to call Gilda for information, what was the point of this memo? All of Sentence 3 and most of Sentence 4 could have been eliminated.

Revision:

Consider the following revision of the Adopt-a-School letter. Analyze why it succeeds where the original fails. Note especially the use of a format (visual organization of printed material via white space, boldface, indentation, bullets, etc.) to make the memo more visually appealing and easier to read.

1) XYZ Company has long been recognized as a company which cares about the community. 2) That reputation is based on the selfless deeds of XYZ employees, beginning with our president, John Smith.

3) People like you have been generous in committing to help others, especially the young people who are our future.

4) Mr. Smith has asked me to tell you about the Adopt-a-School program, which introduces young people to the world of work. 5) We hope XYZ employees will contribute their time to work with high school students. (Even if it's only one hour a month, it will be appreciated.) 6) As an XYZ employee, you know better than anyone else what companies such as ours require for entry-level positions. 7) And that information is what the young people need.

8) Here are some of the ways you might help:

- conduct a half-hour tour of our premises for small groups
- do mailing and make phone calls
- write a press release about the program
- prepare a fact sheet about our company for the students
- speak to small or large groups of students about our firm.

9) If you can participate, please call me at **Extension 113**.

Practice: Analyze these two memos by comparing them to the components of the language of power, as shown on page 61.

Analyze a communication you have recently received. Revise it, using the checklist on page 69, to include the language of power.

Analysis:

Admittedly, the second version is a longer memo, but—because of its thoroughness and specificity—it actually is a more efficient piece of writing. It saves the reader's time by telling her what she needs to know, thus eliminating the additional step of calling Gilda to learn about the program.

The respected leader does not waste the time of her followers. She respects them and what they are trying to accomplish. In the next section, we shall examine how the leader facilitates accomplishment through the language of politics.

Practice: Make a list of power words and another list of words that fail to convey power.

Try writing a commencement address. In it, demonstrate five of the traits noted in the diagram on page 61.

Listen to or read a speech delivered by another power figure. Analyze the language used by that leader as we have done here.

CHECKLIST

☐ Am I using power words in my spoken and written communications?

☐ Do I continually apologize?

☐ Do I over-explain things?

☐ Do I use imperative sentences?

☐ Have I used a format when appropriate?

☐ Am I wasting other people's time?

☐ Have I thought about the placement of my sentences, putting requests for unfavorable information *after* information that explains or validates the request or negative message?

☐ Have I used facts to substantiate my points?

☐ In a longer communication, is there an orderly expression of my thoughts or theme?

☐ Do I use short, familiar, specific words?

☐ Have I avoided careless repetition?

☐ Do I have variety in my sentence structure?

☐ Have I kept my sentences and my paragraphs short?

☐ Have I used the active, rather than the passive, voice?

☐ Have I created the impression that I have (or could have) the support of those who matter?

☐ Have I avoided an accusatory tone?

☐ Have I done my homework so I'm prepared for every outcome?

☐ Might anything in my words come back to haunt me?

☐ Do my communications convey status?

☐ Have I given thought to the next steps to be taken and to the long-range ramifications?

☐ Is this communication one step in a series of strategic, periodic moves to implant and implement my plan?

☐ If I've made a veiled threat, am I prepared to suffer the consequences? (If so, do I realize the strength of that bargaining position?)

☐ Have I displayed the leadership traits evident in Mr. Iacocca's address?

☐ Do I think carefully about the distribution list for each of my written communications?

☐ Have I given thought to psychological motivations?

☐ For a particular memo,

- Is there something I should avoid saying?
- Have I considered what information might strengthen my position and what information might weaken my position?
- Have I checked to determine there is nothing that would offend others?
- Have I used sexist language?
- Is there anything that might be misinterpreted?
- Have I thought twice before putting this in writing, especially if I am angry?

Footnotes

[9] Warren Bennis and Burt Nanus, *Leaders: The Strategies for Taking Charge.* Copyright © 1985 by Bennis and Nanus. Reprinted by permission of Harper & Row, Publishers, Inc., p. 17.

CHAPTER THREE:
The Language of Politics:
A Study of Governor Mario Cuomo's Words

> *Politics is the art of the possible.*
> Bismarck

Introduction

Having the right words and knowing when to use them can make all the difference in the world as far as personal success, cooperative relations and familial harmony are concerned. (Physicians have discovered that people who are able to communicate well have less stress in their lives than others who cannot.)

"Mend your speech a little," Shakespeare urges, "lest it may mar your fortune." Individuals who fail to heed this centuries-old caveat have found themselves flung from the pinnacle of success to the flat plains of failure. Witness the careers of Jimmy "the Greek" Snyder, Al Campanis, Arizona Governor Evan Mecham, to name but a few.

History has been affected, careers have been altered, and battles have been won on the strength of words. Many historians believe that Grover Cleveland, for example, achieved his Presidential victory (and Catholic support) because his Republican opponent unwisely used four words: "Rum, Romanism, and Rebellion." Consider, too, the televised debates between John F. Kennedy and Richard Nixon, or the battle cries which have rallied the nation: "Remember the Maine!" "The war to end all wars!" "Make the world safe for democracy." "Remember Pearl Harbor!"

Leaders—whether in the boardroom or on the battlefield—recognize the importance of being able to influence others with well-chosen words. They recognize the importance of the Job 6:25 reference: "How forcible are right words." Leaders, especially political leaders, know that to convert ideas to reality, the transformation must begin with words.

Tom Peters' View

What separates the mediocre communicator from the memorable one is frequently a simple distinction: the memorable communicator is effective in using words. This point is emphasized by Tom Peters, who—when asked to describe leadership language—replied:

> "The essence of humanness is our language capability. A leader has only his or her language (the language of words *and* consistent, supporting deeds) as a 'tool.' To say that language is everything for the leader is not an overstatement. It is fact."

It is further fact that the elements of leadership language can be studied and successfully applied by anyone who is interested in developing the communications aspect of leadership. In this chapter, we shall examine those elements and then see how they have been applied by New York Governor Mario Cuomo, whose famous Democratic National Convention address reflects attention to both political substance and substance politically stated.

Time magazine recognized the need for political leaders to use language for gaining popular support; in the subtitle of an article about the 1988 Democratic Convention, *Time* observed, "When the pressure was on to prove he could excite as well as manage his party, Dukakis found strength in a new theme: community."[10]

In describing Michael Dukakis' address, *Time* wrote:

> In a speech that had a lilt and a majesty unlike any other he had given in his 16-month quest, Dukakis found the answer.

> "It is the idea of community," he said. "It is the idea that we are in this together; that regardless of who we are or how much money we have—each of us counts." Using the image of community as a contrast to the "cramped ideals" of the Reagan years, he challenged his listeners "to forge a new era of greatness for America."

> Political metaphors are never completely new; like movie scripts, they recycle the heritage of the past. Dukakis traced the

concept of mutual obligation back to the first Massachusetts Governor, John Winthrop, the 17th century embodiment of the Puritan ideal. He could have equally credited Governor Mario Cuomo, who offered the Democrats in 1984 the abiding myth of the nation as an entwined "family."[11]

Style versus Substance

It is this address that we shall examine to find the political elements comprising the *style* of Cuomo's leadership language as well as the political elements comprising the *substance* of Cuomo's leadership language. Such examination requires the reader to analyze on two levels. On the superficial level, we will read for the content of the words, much as you would look at yourself in a mirror. But on a second, deeper level, we will scrutinize the way that content is expressed, just as you would look at the mirror itself—and not your image in it—if you were cleaning that mirror.

If you have ever gone to a movie with someone deeply interested in film, you may have commented on the well-written plot. The film aficionado just might respond with a statement such as this, "Yes, but did you notice the camera angle during the love scene?" He obviously was watching that film on two levels: the surface level of knowing the plot (or understanding the content or looking at yourself in a mirror) and also the deeper level (at which he paid no attention to the substance but just considered the style, or how the substance was conveyed). In the examination of style, substance is relegated to a secondary role, much as you force yourself to ignore your reflected mirror image as you clean.

"If I had to do it all over," reflected former Arizona Governor Evan Mecham, "I would have realized earlier that style is sometimes more important than substance. How things are said is sometimes as important as what is said."

The effective leader recognizes the accuracy of Mecham's observation: *style* is sometimes more important than *substance*. *How* things are said is often as important as *what* is said. The *message*, if not encased in the proper *medium*, will often fail. *Content* is only half a communication: *context* is the other half. *Technical matter* may not be given due consideration if the *technique* for imparting that matter is not appealing to the reader or listener.

All of the following statements were made by individuals in leadership positions; not all of them, however, are expressed in leadership language.

Which do you feel are the words of a true leader?

Josephus Daniels, Secretary of the Navy, in a ceremony of tribute to military women who were about to return to civilian life at the end of World War I: "We will not forget you. As we embraced you in uniform yesterday, we will embrace you without uniform tomorrow."

Robert Spillane, Fairfax County, Virginia school superintendent replying to a reporter's question about the legal controversy concerning a child with AIDS: "The legal action is not necessary because the kid will be dead in a few months."

Neil Bush, son of George Bush, commenting on the following of a rival candidate, "Pat Robertson's supporters are cockroaches issuing from the baseboards of the Bible Belt."

Lee Iacocca, asked to comment on the death of the man who had fired him from Ford Motor Company: "Henry Ford and I were friends for more years than we were enemies."

For both business and political leaders, effective communication is vital. It is not difficult to understand why *Fortune* 500 executives ranked communication skills ahead of other talents when asked the most important quality for business leaders to possess.

Metaphor

In this chapter, we shall investigate the use of stylistic devices employed in the writing of a political leader, New York Governor

Mario Cuomo. Cuomo, in the opening line of his address to the Democratic National Convention, uses a metaphor (a comparison between two things not ordinarily compared) and so establishes his theme of "family":

> "On behalf of the Empire State and the family of New York, I thank you for the great privilege of being allowed to address this convention."

Metaphors bring force and color and imagery to our communications; they allow us to capture, with a single word or phrase, a far-reaching concept. In *Leaders: The Strategies for Taking Charge,* Bennis and Nanus affirm the value of metaphor in leadership language: "A lot of our leaders had a penchant for metaphor if not for models. Comparison, analogy, bring subjects to life."[12]

Jose Ortega y Gasset wrote that "the metaphor is probably the most fertile power possessed by man," a view echoed in *The Leadership Challenge* by James Kouzes and Barry Posner:

> Leaders are also quite attentive to the language used in their organizations. Indeed, this attention focuses on the types of metaphors and analogies used to describe organizational problems and opportunities (that is, critical incidents). Whether the leader likens his or her organization to the tortoise or to the hare has implications about marketing strategies or the importance of new product development. The natural tensions generated by mergers are definitely affected by references to white knights, golden parachutes, greenmail, shark repellents, and war chests. As Tom Peters says, you would not be surprised at receiving poor service from an airline flight attendant whom you overhear remarking just before the passengers board: "Here come the animals!"

Part of the magic of Disney World can be attributed to the deliberate use of language and metaphor. For example, there are no employees at Disneyland, because everyone is a performer. That's why the "personnel department" is called "Central Casting." And in this family-oriented environment, everyone is on a first-name basis, with name badges referring to people as Hosts and Hostesses. And, of course, there are no customers at Disneyland, only Guests (always capitalized) who have come to visit the Magic Kingdom.[13]

We find that Cuomo's metaphoric "family" encapsulates the ideal of unity and weaves that ideal throughout the fabric of the speech:

"In our family are gathered everyone from the abject poor of Essex county in New York, to the enlightened affluent of the gold coasts of both ends of our nation, and in between is the heart of our constituency.

"We believe we must be the family of America, recognizing that at the heart of the matter we are bound to one another, that the problems of a retired school teacher in Duluth are *our* problems.

"We can deal with that deficit intelligently, by shared sacrifice, with all parts of the nation's family contributing, building partnerships with the private sector, providing a sound defense without depriving ourselves of what we need to feed our children and care for our people.

"And that they were able to build a family and live in dignity and see one of their children go from behind their little grocery store on the other side of the tracks in South Jamaica where he was born, to occupy the highest seat in the greatest state of the greatest nation in the only world we know, is an ineffably beautiful tribute to the democratic process."

The speech concludes with a final metaphoric reference to "family":

"I ask you—ladies and gentlemen, brothers and sisters—for the good of all of us, for the love of this great nation, for the family of America, for the love of God. Please, make this nation remember how futures are built."

The "frontier" metaphor is also featured in this address.

"The Republicans believe the wagon train will not make it to the frontier unless some of our old, some of our young, and some of our weak are left behind by the side of the trail.

"We Democrats believe that we can make it all the way with the whole family intact.

"We have. More than once.

"Ever since Franklin Roosevelt lifted himself from his wheel-chair to lift this nation from its knees. Wagon train after wagon train. To new frontiers of education, housing, peace. The whole family aboard. Constantly reaching out to extend and en-large that family. Lifting them up into the wagon on the way. Blacks and Hispanics, people of every ethnic group, and Na-tive Americans—all those struggling to build their families and claim some small share of America."

The metaphor works well to permit mention of a typical political tactic: the inclusion of all kinds of Americans, the embracing of diver-sity to achieve unity, that excellent product emerging from the melting pot which is America.

Practice: 1. Work on being able to express your business philosophy in a metaphoric statement. Or, describe the way your department or division functions by comparing it to something not typically part of the business realm.

2. Assume you have been called upon to deliver an ad-dress about your company. (Your speech will be reprinted in the company newsletter also.) Select a metaphor you could use as a recurrent theme in your speech.

Parallelism

Although we are exploring successful language strategies in the words of an eminent politician, these techniques can be applied to "political" situations within the business realm. Politics, after all, has been defined by Webster's as "competition between competing interest groups of individuals for power and leadership in a government or other group." And, while the word "politics" has a negative connotation for some, the competition to which Webster's alludes need not be negative at all. Those who vie for power and leadership—probably many of you who are reading this book—can and do compete in ways that are totally ethical.

In the Governor's speech, he is clearly helping his party to compete for leadership, the leadership of the nation in this case. Ideally, by exploring Cuomo's leadership language in a political situation, you will be able to apply some of his stylistic devices to office-politics situations.

Another forceful technique is the use of parallel structure. Parallelism simply means that when you are listing a series of items, you should list each item in a consistent fashion. Look at these examples of parallel structure (all emphases added) used by Cuomo to contradict the President's metaphor of a "shining city on a hill."

> "In fact, Mr. President, this nation is more a 'Tale of Two Cities' than it is a 'shining city on a hill.'

> "**Maybe** if you visited more places, Mr. President, you'd understand.

> "**Maybe** if you went to Appalachia where some people still live in sheds, and to Lackawanna where thousands of unemployed steel workers wonder why we subsidize foreign steel while we surrender their dignity to unemployment and to welfare checks.

> "**Maybe** if you stepped into a shelter in Chicago and talked with some of the homeless there.

> "**Maybe**, Mr. President, if you asked a woman who'd been denied the help she needs to feed her children because you say we need the money to give a tax break to a millionaire or to build a missile we can't even afford to use—

"**Maybe** then you'd understand."

The parallelism here is contained in the "Maybe" phrases. Of course, parallelism can be used in a smaller selection, too, such as in this example of parallel structure in prepositional ("by") phrases.

"**By** creating the largest defense budget in history, one even they now admit is excessive. **By** escalating to a frenzy the nuclear arms race. **By** incendiary rhetoric. **By** refusing to discuss peace with our enemies. **By** the loss of 279 young Americans in Lebanon in pursuit of a plan and a policy no one can find or describe."

Again, we find an example in the juxtaposing of two balanced clauses:

"And we will do that **not so much** with speeches that sound good **as with** speeches that are good and sound.

"**Not so much** with speeches that bring people to their feet **as with** speeches that bring people to their senses."

The play on words evident in these two selections is another frequently used aspect of the politician's rhetoric. The clever twisting of familiar phrases ("sound good"/"good and sound") ("people to their feet"/"people to their senses") forces us to consider the words in a fresh, a different way.

Here are other examples of parallelism. Note how effectively Cuomo utilizes the "for..." phrase to envelop multiple sections of his constituency.

"We speak **for the minorities** who have not yet entered the mainstream.

"**For ethnics** who want to add their culture to the mosaic that is America.

"**For women** indignant that we refuse to etch into our governmental commandments the simple rule "Thou shalt not sin against equality."—a commandment so obvious it can be spelled in three letters...E.R.A.

"**For young people** demanding an education and a future.

"**For senior citizens** terrorized by the idea that their only security...their *social* security...is being threatened.

"**For millions of reasoning people** fighting to preserve our environment from greed and stupidity...."

The expletive phrase ("It is") is used here to criticize the administration's deficit spending and to restate the theme of "futures."

"**It is** a deficit that, according to the President's own fiscal advisor, could grow as high as 300 billion dollars a year, stretching as far as the eye can see.

"**It is** a debt so large that as much as one-half of our revenue from the income tax goes to pay the interest on it each year.

"**It is** a mortgage on our children's futures that can only be paid in pain and that could eventually bring this nation to its knees."

Humor

The subsequent line evinces the humor to which audiences respond so well:

"Don't take my word for it...I'm a Democrat."

Practice: 1. Pay attention the next time you read or hear an address, especially a political one. Make note of the parallel structures employed.

Also note parallelism or lack of it in the business communications you encounter daily. For example, this job-description sentence is not parallel in its structure.

The responsibilities for this position include overseeing the office staff, implementing management policies, preparing monthly activity reports and variance reports, and the supervision of all employees involved in purchasing.

The last item should have read "supervising all employees involved in purchasing."

One note of caution is in order here. Parallelism is not to be confused with careless repetition. The writer who starts nine out of ten sentences with the word "The" is probably unaware of the dullness produced by such repetition. Variety in sentence structure is needed in this case if the writer is to capture the interest of his audience.

Parallelism, however, is a deliberate syntactical repetition for the purposes of emphasizing or producing an attracting cadence.

2. Take any five of the following cliches (many of which are metaphorical expressions) and try to bring new life to them by adding a fresh verbal twist as Cuomo did with the "sound good/good and sound" and the "people to their feet/people to their senses" references. Use your newly created expressions in appropriate future communications or speeches, especially those designed to inspire.

add insult to injury	hard row to hoe
all in a day's work	have a foot in the door
all things being equal	hit the nail on the head
as luck would have it	hook, line, and sinker
at a loss for words	in the final analysis
axe to grind	in the long run
bark up the wrong tree	in the nick of time
beat around the bush	irons in the fire
bend over backward	jig is up

benefit of the doubt

better late than never

bite off more than you can chew

bite the bullet

bone of contention

bring home the bacon

burn the midnight oil

can't see the forest for the trees

checkered career

chip off the old block

cool as a cucumber

diamond in the rough

do your own thing

down in the dumps

down your alley

draw the line

easier said than done

face the music

far be it from me

fate worse than death

feather in your cap

feeling your oats

few and far between

flash in the pan

food for thought

foot in your mouth

get down to brass tacks

goes without saying

handwriting on the wall

keep a low profile

knock on wood

last but not least

lean and hungry look

leave in the lurch

leave no stone unturned

left-handed compliment

let your hair down

let the cat out of the bag

like a house on fire

long arm of the law

mad as a wet hen

mad dash

make ends meet

make no bones about it

method in your madness

more than meets the eye

needle in a haystack

never a dull moment

never rains but it pours

never say die

nip it in the bud

none the worse for wear

no sooner said than done

once in a blue moon

other side of the coin

over a barrel

perfect gentleman

play it by ear

3. Begin to collect humorous references, quotations, anecdotes, or lines that would be appropriate in communications situations that require you to "compete for power and leadership of a group."

Tone

The tone of your communications will, of course, affect the attitude with which your audience receives your message. For a communication of considerable length, the tone may undergo subtle shifts, but there will generally be one prevalent strain or mood throughout.

Strive for an acceptable tone in your own writing. While there are times when a firm, no-nonsense approach is required, you will need to avoid seeming autocratic. Never indulge the tendency for sarcasm in your written communications; not only will you alienate the target of your remarks but you will also alienate others whose sympathy will have been piqued.

In a similar vein, excessive humility usually fails to win over your audience. No one respects a leader who does not feel (or pretends not to feel) that she is worthy of respect or praise. We follow those leaders who have proven they are better than the average. For such a person to belittle her own accomplishments causes others to doubt the leader's sincerity *or* competence.

Today's audiences, thanks to the advent of television, are fairly sophisticated listeners. They have seen and heard the best and so are knowledgeable (if only through observation) about leadership language that succeeds. Obvious flattery will estrange your readers or listeners; they will feel you are appealing to their vanity rather than to their minds.

A condescending tone will cause listeners or readers to turn away from your message almost immediately. Business people are often unaware of the potential for insult in seemingly innocuous phrases such as "you people," "I cannot permit," "may I suggest," "in my experience," et cetera. You may indeed feel superior to those you are addressing, but if your speech reveals that feeling, you are bound to lose your following.

Division, rather than unity, is created by the leader who adopts a preachy tone. The speaker or writer who suggests an "I" rather than a "we" attitude is really suggesting that he alone knows what needs to be done. While we do turn to leaders for motivation, inspiration, and guidance, we need to feel that we, too, have some contribution to make to the overall mission.

Governor Cuomo's tone is authoritative, business-like, matter-of-fact, but never condescending or preachy. From the onset, we can virtually see him roll up his shirt sleeves and plunge into the task before him. Note the second and third sentences of his speech:

"Please allow me to skip the stories and the poetry and the temptation to deal in nice but vague rhetoric.

"Let me instead use this valuable opportunity to deal with the questions that should determine this election and that are vital to the American people."

The simplicity of certain expressions add to that impression of strength and authority:

"Some of us are in this room today only because this nation had that confidence. It would be wrong to forget that."

"We must win this case on the merits."

"We're proud of that diversity.... But we pay a price for it."

We respect those leaders wise enough to know what is wrong, or at least to take a stand and point out that the emperor has no clothes. Note how Cuomo at first acquiesces and then attacks in this excerpt:

"The President said he didn't understand that fear. He said, 'Why, this country is a shining city on a hill.'

"The President is right. In many ways, we *are* 'a shining city on a hill.'

"But the hard truth is that not everyone is sharing in this city's splendor and glory."

Practice: 1. For the next important business communication you have to prepare, decide in advance the tone you wish to achieve. Then experiment with various phrases to see which best convey the impression you wish to have your audience receive.

2. Analyze a recent memo you have written or received. What tone is prevalent? Is the tone selected the appropriate one for the content and for the audience? If the memo does not succeed in conveying leadership language, determine which words and phrases created a negative impression or tone.

Variety in Sentence Length

Another effective technique in delivering a political speech or handling business correspondence is to have variety in the length of your sentences. Your sentences should *average* fifteen words.

If your sentences are so long that the reader has to go back to the beginning of the sentence because he forgot what it said, then he cannot read efficiently. Linguists have found that sentences that have more than twenty or twenty-five words are difficult to read for this very reason.

So, while you should aim for a readable average number of words per sentence, you should also incorporate a variety of sentence lengths to keep your reader interested.

Look at the various sentence lengths in this one paragraph from the Governor's speech:

"The Republicans called it trickle-down when Hoover tried it. Now they call it supply side. It is the same shining city for those relative few who are lucky enough to live in its good neighborhoods."

Practice: Examine a memo or report you recently wrote. Do you have any excessively long sentences? Do you have variety in the length of your sentences? If not, pledge to bring such variety to your future communications.

Variety in Sentence Structure

Writers and speakers who use the same basic sentence structure over and over again run the risk of boring their audience. Just as you would quickly become disenchanted with a task—no matter how intriguing it initially was—that you had to perform thirty times in a row, so, too will your reader or listener fail to be stirred by a carelessly repetitive pattern. The most common structure or sentence pattern is the subject-verb-direct object order. Here are some alternatives.

Adverb

Try using an adverb at the beginning of your sentences. (Adverbs modify verbs and tell "how," "when," and "where." They also modify other adverbs and adjectives by telling "to what extent.")

"**Today** our great Democratic Party, which has saved this nation from depression, from Fascism, from racism, from corruption, is called upon to do it again."

Expletive

An occasional expletive (used in the syntactical sense and not the Nixonian) will lend interest to your sentence structure. Expletives are essentially filler phrases which do not add significantly to the meaning of the thought. Such expressions as "it is" or "there are" or "there is" can be used, though, on occasion as an option to the subject-verb-direct object order.

"**There are** elderly people who tremble in the basements of the houses there.

"**There are** people who sleep in the city's streets, in the gutter, where the glitter doesn't show.

"**There are** ghettos where thousands of young people, without an education or a job, give their lives away to drug dealers every day."

Prepositions

Again, for variety's sake, you can alter your basic sentence pattern by beginning some sentences with a preposition, such as "for" or "in."

"**For** nearly fifty years we carried them to new levels of comfort, security, dignity, even affluence."

"**In** order to succeed, we must answer our opponent's polished and appealing rhetoric with a more telling reasonableness and rationality."

Infinitive phrase

Another variation that will keep your audience's attention is the use of an infinitive phrase. (An infinitive is a verb form which has the word "to" in front of the verb.) Cuomo employs such a structure in the following:

"**To succeed**, we will have to surrender small parts of our individual interests, to build a platform we can *all* stand on, at once, comfortably—proudly singing out the truth for the nation to hear, in chorus, its logic so clear and commanding that no slick commercial, no amount of geniality, no martial music will be able to muffle it."

Verb

Imperative sentences—those that begin with a verb—have the ring of authority. Note the forcefulness and vigor in these examples of leadership language:

"**Ask** them what they think of our economy, now that it has been driven by the distorted value of the dollar back to its colonial condition—exporting agricultural products and importing manufactured ones."

"**Think** about it: what chance would the Republican candidate have had in 1980 if he had told the American people that he intended to pay for his so-called economic recovery with bankruptcies, unemployment and the largest debt known to humankind?"

"**Remember**, fifty years of progress never cost us what the last four years of stagnation have."

"**Let** me instead use this valuable opportunity to deal with the questions that should determine this election and that are vital to the American people."

Dependent clause

Words like "if," "when," "since" are used to connect subordinate or dependent clauses with the main idea or independent clause. This stylistic device of subordination is useful for emphasizing one idea over the other. It is also useful for bringing diversity to the usual sentence pattern.

"**If we need any inspiration to make the effort to put aside our small differences**, all we need to do is to reflect on the Republican policy of divide and cajole and how it has injured our land since 1980."

"**If they're not too embarrassed to tell you the truth**, they'll say they are appalled and frightened by the President's deficit."

Practice: 1. Think about a business communication you must prepare soon. State the purpose of that communication by answering the following (on a separate sheet of paper):

In this memo, I want to tell someone that _____
_____.

Now restate the information in the blank space by writing two different sentences using two different sentence structure variations.

2. Identify which structures these sentences (from Iacocca's address to the National Governors' Association) employ.

"Today, I see 50 states fighting for jobs."

"There are plenty of practicing ideologues in Washington, but not in Lansing, or Columbus, or Springfield or the other state capitals."

"As governors, you've got to be pragmatic."

"By the way, at the same time I saw our own labor unions resisting productivity changes in our *old* plants, but cutting any deal it took to represent employees at any *new* plant financed by foreign capital."

"While we've been debating, we've been losing the economic war."

"Come on down to Detroit when you're through here, and I'll take you through some auto plants that are as modern and efficient as anything they've got in Japan or anywhere else."

Vision

Leaders are able to rise above their mundane involvements and grasp "the big picture." They bring meaning to the flood of information which circulates in any organization. Rather than being swept along on these wave crests of data, rather than being inundated with facts, they manage to create understanding of purpose by creating a vision.

Peter Drucker, father of modern management science, observed that the real challenge for business people is to get communication out of information. In a similar vein, Bennis and Nanus observe:

Leaders articulate and define what has previously remained implicit or unsaid; then they invent images, metaphors, and models that provide a focus for new attention. By so doing, they consolidate or challenge prevailing wisdom. In short, an *essential* factor in leadership is the capacity to influence and *organize meaning* for the members of the organization.[14]

As we have noted, politics—in the most common sense of the word—means a struggle for leadership. To lead in political situations, especially those in the corporate realm, one must be able to create a vision for others.

Cuomo effectively uses President Reagan's vision of a shining city on a hill to expose the underbelly of that city, thereby creating another vision which he hopes will move his audience to vote in favor of his party.

"A shining city is perhaps all the President sees from the portico of the White House and the veranda of his ranch, where everyone seems to be doing well.

"But there's another part of the city, the part where some people can't pay their mortgages and most young people can't afford one, where students can't afford the education they need and middle-class parents watch the dreams they hold for their children evaporate.

"In this part of the city there are more poor than ever, more families in trouble, more and more people who need help but can't find it.

"Even worse: there are elderly people who tremble in the basements of the houses there. There are people who sleep in the city's streets, in the gutter, where the glitter doesn't show. There are ghettos where thousands of young people, without an education or a job, give their lives away to drug dealers every day."

The refutation of his opponent's image is carefully constructed: there are concrete examples, graphic references, disturbing microcosmic images of the macrocosmic world which frightens us all.

Practice: 1. Think about your organization and try to define, as Bennis and Nanus suggest, something that has been implicit. Go ahead and formulate an image or a vision that you would like others to share. Organize the meaning of your firm's purpose. (Note: do *not* use the image of the family or of the shining/non-shining city.)

2. Speak to business people outside your firm. Ask them what their company's vision is. Try to speak to individuals fairly high in the hierarchy, as such individuals are usually the ones responsible for articulating that vision.

3. Read the annual reports of several different companies. See if you can find a clearly articulated vision in the overviews presented.

Questions

To pique the concern of your audience, to force them to think about the issues you are raising, you should present a question from time to time. This stylistic technique can be used as you write a meeting's agenda or as you prepare a speech.

Governor Cuomo punctuates his remarks with strategically placed questions such as these:

"Where would another four years take us?"

"How much larger will the deficit be?"

"How much deeper the cuts in programs for the struggling middle class and the poor to limit that deficit?"

"How high the interest rates?"

"How much deeper will be the gulf between us and our enemies?"

"Will we make meaner the spirit of our people?"

"How high will we pile the missiles?"

Practice: For the next important business communication you
have to prepare, begin with some questions you would
like to have your audience consider. Then, use those
questions as strategic threads in the fabric of your
memo, report, letter or presentation.

Alliteration

Politicians are fond of using alliterative phrases—ones in which
several words begin with the same letter. Alliterative sentences are better known by children as tongue-twisters: "Peter Piper picked a
peck...."

This stylistic device, however, is used by numerous leaders to
make their words more memorable, to make them stand out. As a rule,
alliterative phrases have an attracting ring to them, but if used to excess, they can cause your language to sound less than professional.

Here we have two important words emphasized through alliteration: repetition of the letter "c":

"The difference between Democrats and Republicans has
always been measured in courage and confidence."

And here with the letter "l" and then the letter "r":

Surely the Republicans won't bring the convention together.
Their policies divide the nation into the lucky and the left-out,
the royalty and the rabble.

And in this phrase with the letter "m":

no martial music will be able to muffle it.

Practice: Over the next several days, look for alliterative phrases
used in advertising, in corporate communications and in
presentations made by leaders whom you respect.

Personification

As the word suggests, personification is the process of assigning human attributes to non-living things. To illustrate, if we say that the sun danced on the waves, we have actually personified the sun. It does not have legs so it cannot dance in a literal sense. And yet, figuratively speaking, the words create a distinct picture of sunshine glittering on the white foam of waves.

In this example, Cuomo personifies the word "nation," treating it as if it were a single corporeal entity. (Note the similarity in theme between the following, and remarks made by Lee Iacocca in the preceding chapter.)

"It is a mortgage on our children's future that can only be paid in pain and that could eventually bring this nation to its knees."

Again, the concept of a nation is personified with the word "knees":

"Ever since Franklin Roosevelt lifted himself from his wheelchair to lift this nation from its knees."

In this next case, an unwillingness to compromise is regarded as a person, capable of discussion:

"...a macho intransigence that refuses to make intelligent attempts to discuss the possibility of nuclear holocaust with our enemy...."

Practice: 1. In Ronald Reagan's Inaugural Address at the end of this chapter, you will find numerous examples of personification, such as this one:

"Government, the people said, was not our master, it is our servant; its only power will be that which we the people allow it to have."

The noun "government" is an abstract concept. Granted, a government is composed of individuals, but to treat the concept as if it were a single person—

a master or a servant—is to employ personification. Find other examples of well-chosen personification in the former President's speech.

2. Look for examples of all the other stylistic devices discussed in this chapter as you read the Inaugural Address of this great leader. In the first five paragraphs alone, you will find examples of variety in sentence structure and sentence length, alliteration, the use of supporting details, transitions, and the creation of an image.

Cohesion

A well-crafted communication, like a well-structured building, has been carefully developed. Each piece is carefully aligned with the next to achieve a tight fit of the building blocks. Similarly, you can attain such cohesion in your writing by repeating the underlying themes at pivotal points. We see Governor Cuomo doing this with his numerous allusions to family unity and to the future.

Another way to achieve tightness in your communications is to use transitional devices. Transitions are the bridges that lead us from one idea to the next. You may regard them as the verbal glue that binds our thoughts together.

A transition might be a single word, a phrase or even a whole sentence. In longer documents, the transition might be a whole paragraph or even a whole page.

In these excerpts, we see how Cuomo's references to "division" tie these two paragraphs together:

"We Democrats must unite so that the entire nation can. Surely the Republicans won't bring the convention together. Their policies **divide** the nation....

"The Republicans are willing to treat **that division** as victory. They would cut this nation in half, into those temporarily better off and those worse off than before, and call it recovery."

Here are some common transitions. Incorporate them into future messages so that your language will reflect the tight, logical organization we expect of our leaders.

Addition:	again, also, besides, further, too, moreover, in addition, additionally
Comparison and Contrast:	after all, however, by comparison, similarly, by contrast, still
Results:	consequently, hence, thus, ergo, therefore, accordingly
Example or Emphasis:	for example, as has been stated, in fact, indeed, in particular, of course
Purpose:	to this end, with this goal in mind, for this purpose, toward this objective
Time:	traditionally, ordinarily, in the meantime, presently, usually

Practice: Go back and examine a long communication you recently prepared. Have you used transitional devices? If not, look for places where you could insert them to bring unity and a logical flow to your thoughts.

Refutation

A good debater knows that she cannot avoid an opponent's likely arguments. Instead, the skilled debater anticipates those arguments, examines them, and then refutes them. By comparison, a good political communicator knows the importance of considering the opposition's stand and then undermining that stand with deliberate, specific thrusts.

This ploy is exemplified in the following as the Governor uses his opponent's very words:

"The President has asked us to judge him on whether or not he's fulfilled the promises he made four years ago.

"I accept that. Just consider what he said and what he's done.

"Inflation is down since 1980. But not because of the supply-side miracle promised by the President. Inflation was reduced the old-fashioned way, with a recession, the worst since 1932. More than 55,000 bankruptcies. Two years of massive unemployment. 200,000 farmers and ranchers forced off the land. More homeless than at any other time since the Great Depression. More hungry, more poor—mostly women—and a nearly 200 billion-dollar deficit threatening our future."

Practice: Think about your competition, preferably a competitive firm in your industry. Take a statement (perhaps an advertising slogan) and attempt to invalidate your opponent's claims by using specific details to oppose or contradict those claims.

Anecdote

In a well-known study involving MBA students, Martin and Powers[15] attempted to persuade students that a particular company was committed to avoiding layoffs. The four techniques used were telling a story, using statistics, using the story plus statistics, and finally, sharing a policy statement issued by the company. The students in the group who were given only the story believed the claim more than students in any of the other groups.

The study suggests the power of anecdotes and in the next chapter, you will find a similar view expressed by Tom Peters. But now, let us turn to an experience about the Governor's life to see what a powerful effect real-life stories can have upon an audience.

"That struggle to live with dignity is the real story of the shining city. It's a story I didn't read in a book, or learn in a classroom. I saw it, and lived it. Like many of you.

"I watched a small man with thick calluses on both hands work fifteen and sixteen hours a day. I saw him once literally bleed from the bottoms of his feet, a man who came here uneducated, alone, unable to speak the language, who taught me all I needed to know about faith and hard work by the simple eloquence of his example. I learned about our kind of democracy from my father. I learned about our obligation to each other from him and from my mother. They asked only for a chance to work and to make the world better for their children and to be protected in those moments when they would not be able to protect themselves. This nation and its government did that for them.

"And that they were able to build a family and live in dignity and see one of their children go from behind their little grocery store on the other side of the tracks in South Jamaica where he was born, to occupy the highest seat in the greatest state of the greatest nation in the only world we know, is an ineffably beautiful tribute to the democratic process."

Throughout this chapter, we have encouraged you to employ certain stylistic devices as you work to maintain or strengthen your political position. Speaking and writing as well as this politician does is no easy task. But, it is an achievable task.

By studying the precise elements of leadership language, you will be prepared to take the next step: using those elements in situations calling for you to be a leader. With sufficient analysis and practice, you can achieve the task and accomplish the goal of speaking and writing as well as the leaders in this book do.

Use the checklist on the next page to periodically remind yourself of the elements of leadership language.

CHECKLIST

☐ Have I made metaphorical comparisons when appropriate?

☐ Have I employed parallel structure?

☐ Has humor been used on occasion in my addresses?

☐ Is the tone a correct one for the content and for the audience?

☐ Do my sentences reflect variety in both length and structure?

☐ Have I articulated my own vision of my company's purpose? Have I made others aware of it?

☐ Are questions used from time to time in my corporate communications?

☐ Can I create, when a special emphasis is needed, an alliterative phrase?

☐ Do I fully understand what a powerful image can be created by personification? Do I have at least one such image available in reference to my firm?

☐ Are transitions used to tie ideas together?

☐ As a rule, do I anticipate the objections others will have and then address those potential sources of conflict?

☐ Do I rely exclusively on factual matter when attempting to persuade others, or do I have an appropriate anecdote I can use to illustrate that same information?

The Second Inaugural Address of Ronald Reagan, President of the United States, delivered on January 21, 1985*

There are no words adequate to express my thanks for the great honor you have bestowed on me. I will do my utmost to be deserving of your trust.

This is, as Senator Mathias told us, the 50th time that we the people have celebrated this historic occasion. When the first President, George Washington, placed his hand upon the Bible, he stood less than a single day's journey by horseback from raw, untamed wilderness. There were 4 million Americans in a Union of 13 states. Today, we are 60 times as many in a Union of 50 states.

We have lighted the world with our inventions, gone to the aid of mankind wherever in the world there was a cry for help, journeyed to the moon and safely returned. So much has changed. And yet, we stand together as we did two centuries ago.

When I took this oath four years ago, I did so in a time of economic stress. Voices were raised saying that we had to look to our past for greatness and glory. But we, the present-day Americans, are not given to looking backward. In this blessed land, there is always a better tomorrow.

Four years ago, I spoke to you of a new beginning and we have accomplished that. But in another sense, our new beginning is a continuation of that beginning created two centuries ago when, for the first time in history, government, the people said, was not our master, it is our servant; its only power will be that which we the people allow it to have. That system never failed us. But for a time, we failed the system.

* Reprinted with permission.

We asked things of government that government was not equipped to give. We yielded authority to the national government that properly belonged to the states or to local governments or to the people themselves. We allowed taxes and inflation to rob us of our earnings and savings, and watched the great industrial machine that had made us the most productive people on Earth slow down and the number of unemployed increase. By 1980, we knew it was time to renew our faith; to strive with all our strength toward the ultimate freedom, consistent with an orderly society. We believed then and now: There are no limits to growth and human progress, when men and women are free to follow their dreams. And we were right to believe that. Tax rates have been reduced, inflation cut dramatically and more people are employed than ever before in our history.

My fellow citizens, our nation is posed for greatness. We must do what we know is right, and do it with all our might. Let history say of us, these were golden years—when the American Revolution was reborn, when freedom gained new life and America reached for her best.

Two of our founding Fathers, a Boston Lawyer named Adams and a Virginia planter named Jefferson, members of that remarkable group who met in Independence Hall and dared to think they could start the world over again, left us an important lesson. They had become, in the years spent in government, bitter political rivals. In the Presidential election of 1800, and then years later when both were retired and age had softened their anger, they began to speak to each other again through letters. A bond was re-established between those two who had helped create this government of ours.

In 1826, the 50th anniversary of the Declaration of Independence, they both died. They died on the same day, within a few hours of each other. And that day was the Fourth of July. In one of those letters exchanged in the sunset of their lives, Jefferson wrote, "It carries me back to the times when, beset with difficulties and dangers, we were fellow laborers in the same cause, struggling for what is most valuable to man, his right of self-government. Laboring always at the same oar, with some wave ever ahead threatening to overwhelm us, and yet passing harmless...we rode through the storm with heart and hand."

Well, with heart and hand, let us stand as one today: One people under God determined that our future shall be worthy of our past. We must never again abuse the trust of working men and women by sending their earnings on a futile chase after the spiraling demands of a bloated federal establishment.

You elected us in 1980 to end this prescription for disaster. And I don't believe you re-elected us in 1984 to reverse course. At the heart of our efforts is one idea vindicated by 25 straight months of economic growth: Freedom and incentives unleash the drive and entrepreneurial genius that are the core of human progress. We have begun to increase the rewards for work, savings and investment, reduce the increase in the cost and size of government and its interference in people's lives.

We must simplify our tax system, make it more fair and bring the rates down for all who work and earn. A dynamic economy, with more citizens working and paying taxes, will be our strongest tool to bring down budget deficits. But an almost unbroken 50 years of deficit spending has finally brought us to a time of reckoning. We have come to a turning point, a moment for hard decisions. I have asked the Cabinet and my staff a question and now I put the same question to all of you. If not us, who? And, if not now, when? It must be done by all of us going forward with a program aimed at reaching a balanced budget. We can then begin reducing the national debt.

I will shortly submit a budget to the Congress aimed at freezing government program spending for the next year. Beyond this, we must take further steps to permanently control government's power to tax and spend. We must act now to protect future generations from government's desire to spend its citizens' money and tax them into servitude when the bills come due. Let us make it unconstitutional for the federal government to spend more than the federal government takes in. There is a place for the federal government in matters of social compassion. But our fundamental goals must be to reduce dependency and upgrade the dignity of those who are infirm or disadvantaged.

There is another area where the federal government can play a part. As an older American, I remember a time when people of different race, creed or ethnic origin in our land found hatred and prejudice installed in social custom and, yes, in law. Let us resolve that we the people will build an American opportunity society, in which all of us—white and black, rich and poor, young and old—will go forward together, arm in arm. Again, let us remember that, though our heritage is one of bloodlines from every corner of the Earth, we are all Americans pledged to carry on this last, best hope of man on Earth.

Let me turn now to a task that is the primary responsibility of national government—the safety and security of our people. Today, we utter no prayer more fervently than the ancient prayer for peace on Earth. Yet history has shown that peace does not come, nor will our freedom be preserved by good will alone. There are those in the world who scorn our vision of human dignity and freedom. One nation, the Soviet Union, has conducted the greatest military buildup in the history of man, building arsenals of awesome, offensive weapons. We have made progress in restoring our defense capability. But much remains to be done.

There is only one way safely and legitimately to reduce the cost of national security, and that is to reduce the need for it. And this we are trying to do in negotiations with the Soviet Union. We are not just discussing limits on a further increase of nuclear weapons. We seek, instead, to reduce their number. We seek total elimination, one day, of nuclear weapons from the face of the earth.

We strive for peace and security, heartened by the changes all around us. Since the turn of the century, the number of democracies in the world has grown fourfold. Human freedom is on the march, and nowhere more so than in our own hemisphere. Freedom is one of the deepest and noblest aspirations of the human spirit. People worldwide hunger for the right of self-determination, for those inalienable rights that make for human dignity and progress.

America must remain freedom's staunchest friend, for freedom is our best ally. And it is the world's only hope to conquer poverty and preserve peace. Every blow we inflict against poverty will be a blow against its dark allies of oppression and war. Every victory for human freedom will be a victory for world peace.

So we go forward today, a nation still mighty in its youth and powerful in its purpose. With our alliances strengthened, with our economy leading the world to a new age of economic expansion, we look to a future rich in possibilities. And all of this is because we worked and acted together, not as members of political parties, but as Americans. My friends, we live in a world lit by lightning. So much is changing and will change, but so much endures and transcends time.

May God continue to hold us close as we fill the world with our sound—in unity, affection, and love. One people under God, dedicated to the dream of freedom He has placed in the human heart, called upon now to pass that dream on to a waiting and a hopeful world.

God bless you and may God bless America.

Footnotes

[10] "The Duke of Unity," by Walter Shapiro. *Time*, August 1, 1988. Copyright © 1988, Time Inc. Reprinted by permission, p. 14.

[11] Ibid., p. 15.

[12] Bennis, op. cit., p. 35.

[13] Kouzes, James M., and Barry Z. Posner, *The Leadership Challenge* (San Francisco: Jossey-Bass Publishers, 1987), p. 207.

[14] Bennis, op. cit., p. 39.

[15] Martin, J., and Powers, M., "Organizational Stories: More Vivid and Persuasive than Quantitative Data." In B.M. Staw (ed.) *Psychological Foundations of Organizational Behavior*. Glenview, Ill.: Scott, Foresman, 1982, pp. 161–168.

CHAPTER FOUR:
The Language of Persuasion:
A Study of Tom Peters' Words

> *Leadership appears to be the art of getting others to want to do something that you are convinced should be done.*
> Vance Packard

Introduction

No art is more important to you as a leader than persuading others to share your conviction, to dream your dream, to work as hard as you are willing to work to accomplish a goal. It has been said that only the persuaded can persuade; it is this conviction to which Packard alludes above.

Leadership cannot exist without "followership"; to help others carry out your concept of a mission requires persuasion, preferably of the gentle type.

Practice: What is *your* definition of leadership? How does it compare with the generally accepted definition above?

Cuomo's Definition

When asked what constitutes the language of leadership, Governor Cuomo replied:

"The language of leadership involves the expression of ideas in such persuasive manner as to move large numbers of people to support those ideas for the benefit of society."

His words parallel those of management experts who have researched the area of leadership. Warren Bennis and Burt Nanus, for example, echo the importance of persuasion skills for today's leaders. They assert,

Many people have rich and deeply textured agendas, but without communication nothing will be realized. Success requires the capacity to relate a compelling image of a desired state of affairs—the kind that induces enthusiasm and commitment in others.

How do you capture imaginations? How do you communicate visions? How do you get people aligned behind overarching goals? How do you get an audience to recognize and accept an idea? Workers have to recognize and get behind something of established identity. The management of meaning, mastery of communication, is inseparable from effective leadership.[16]

Leaders make us wish to follow them, to pledge our fidelity to them, to sacrifice some of our private goals to help them accomplish more public goals. The leader, above all else, is able to recognize, to acknowledge, and to emphasize duty—not duty in the sense of task but duty in the sense of challenge. The leader makes the prospect of this challenge so enticing that we want to offer our time and our skills to aid in effecting the change she believes is necessary. The leader urges us to climb on the bandwagon and to drink from the communal cup of anticipated success.

When John F. Kennedy asked Americans to give up the comforts of civilized American life and work with the less fortunate in underprivileged Peach Corps countries, he manifested this all-important aspect of leadership: the ability to assure others that pursuit of the leader's goals is more worthy than pursuit of the follower's individual interests. (We find that same admixture of satisfaction and sacrifice in the current advertisement for the Peace Corps: "The toughest job you'll ever love.")

Paradoxically, the leader does not always say the popular thing. Note these words from Governor Cuomo's diaries:

That leaves the politician with choices. Go along with the dominant trend and try to give the people all that they want to assure yourself popularity, enough to win the chance to serve. Then continue to behave that way in order to continue to earn the right to continue to serve. That's "good politics": it wins.

Another choice is to try to lead—at least in opinion—by pointing to what you think is a better way. This requires disagreeing with the people's dominant opinions from time to time and trying to convince them they are wrong. This is risky politics, and today it does not appear to succeed often, but it's the only kind of politics I'm comfortable with.

What is clear is that it is not just risky but suicidal, politically, to disagree with prevailing opinion and not to offer alternatives.[17]

Those who have heard the Governor speak on controversial issues know that he is a man of his words. He declines to take the comfortable middle-of-the-road position on difficult issues; instead, he is brave enough and secure enough to tell supporters and dissenters alike what he believes, which is not necessarily what they wish to hear.

The trait can be identified in numerous other leaders, including all the Presidents in recent memory. Leaders know that they have been chosen (in some cases, self-appointed) to get a job done and not to win a popularity contest.

Defined by Iacocca

Lee Iacocca responded to the question, "What, in your opinion, constitutes the language of leadership?" in the following way:

Strong words

"Strong, simple words that tell people things they don't want to hear. It's a leader's job to bring the bad news, to get people to believe things they don't want to believe and then to go out and do things they don't want to do."

Iacocca exemplifies his opinion as he defines it. Note the selection of strong, simple words that remind those of us who would be leaders that we must sometimes oppose prevalent views, as both he and the Governor maintain.

Simple words

Simple words are direct, familiar, everyday expressions. Sometimes called "first-degree" words, they convey immediate meaning. A non-leader parent might say to a child at bedtime, "Scintillate, scintillate, asteroid minific." The parent who values the strength of simplicity, however, would say instead, "Twinkle, twinkle, little star."

Short words

Should you doubt the truth of this assertion, be reminded of the advice of Dennis Roth: "If it takes a lot of words to say what you have in mind, give it more thought." Think back to Ernest Hemingway's works and the verbal economy which led him to the Nobel Prize for Literature. Strong words are short words. "Sesquipedalian" or "polysyllabic" words usually lack the crispness afforded by simple, familiar words.

Specific words

Specific words will also be stronger than words that are vague. Double-speakers often opt for ambiguous or euphemistic words to avoid the clarity which comes from saying exactly what you mean. Followers should know exactly what their leader is talking about. They shouldn't have to guess at the leader's intended meaning. Can you tell—with just one reading—what this 155-word sentence from an actual corporation's letter to stockholders is saying?

> In order to provide adequately for discretion in the Board of Directors of the Corporation with respect to providing non-contributory and contributory pension for employees under varying circumstances as occasion may require, it is considered necessary, as set forth in the attached plan for employee pension benefits, to continue the authority of the Board of Directors of the Corporation to authorize adoption of the pension provisions and benefits so as to provide different pension benefits of employee contributions from those set forth, to provide for the same or different benefits for other groups of employees, and to designate employees as being within or no

longer within the coverage of any such pension benefits, all as the Board of Directors of the Corporation shall, in its discretion, from time to time believe to be required by the differing situations of various employees or groups of employees and in the best interests of the Corporation and its stockholders.

Or this *single* sentence from the standard contract form of a well-known manufacturing firm:

Notwithstanding any other provisions of this Order, including but not limited to the provision of the clauses of this Order entitled "Changes" and "Termination," (1) Seller shall not be bound to continue performance, incur costs or obligations or take any other action in connection with this Order, including any changes thereto pursuant to the clause of this Order entitled "Changes," which would cause the total amount which Buyer would otherwise be obligated to pay Seller, in the event of completion, termination for convenience of Buyer pursuant to the clause hereunder entitled "Termination," or otherwise to exceed the sum allotted then set forth in this Order, and (2) Buyer shall not be obligated to pay Seller for any costs or obligations or any other actions taken by Seller in connection with this Order, including any changes thereto pursuant to the clause of this Order entitled "Changes," which in the event of completion, termination for convenience of Buyer pursuant to the clause of this Order entitled "Termination," or otherwise, any amount in excess of the sum allotted then set forth in this Order, unless and until Buyer shall have notified Seller in writing and to the extent the sum allotted set forth in the Order is increased.

Clearly, such is not the language of leaders...the language of lawyers, perhaps, but not the language of leaders.

Suitable words

Leaders know that to reach a given individual or group, they must use words that are appropriate to the audience and to the situation. As listeners or readers, we are more likely to be persuaded by words that have significance for us than by words that are not proper or relevant.

Sharp words

Words can cut. Leaders use words with a cutting edge to carve away the pomposity which often bloats a simple message. "It is the belief of this writer that the implementation of the policy, recently formulated by the director of this company, is essential for the furtherance of the economic future of this company" lacks the crispness of this same-message sentence: "We must implement the director's policy."

Leadership language reflects Thomas Jefferson's assertion: "The most valuable of all talents is that of never using two words when one will do."

Surprise words

The words to which we pay attention are those which capture our attention. Yes, we should use familiar words and yes, we should use simple and common words. However, on occasion, we need to startle our audience or surprise them with the unexpected. The surprise words need not be big words (although big words do add verbal spice sometimes), but they should be unexpected words that will pique an audience's interest. (In the Governor's speech he referred to a policy of "divide and cajole"; the phrase really captures our attention because we were expecting, of course, the usual "divide and conquer.")

Listen to the strong, simple words Iacocca uses to tell an audience (The National Governors' Association, in this case) what they may not want to hear, in order to get them to do things they may not want to do.

> "I'll have to say, though, that some governors seem to forget everything they learned while they were governors once they get to Washington—especially the part about balancing budgets! They always blame it on defense, of course, or the Congress. I think we're getting used to the idea in this country that defense is something we *need*, but something we don't have to *pay for*. We just sort of put it on the tab. As for Congress, the current fashion in Washington seems to be to pretend it's just not there.

"Something else that certain governors seem to forget about when they go to Washington is *competing*!"

Change is usually preceded by criticism, a stimulus that propels people to action. We hear that criticism in Iacocca's observation:

"Today, I see 50 states fighting for jobs. But a funny thing: I don't see that same kind of fighting spirit in Washington."

The tone becomes even harsher:

"There are plenty of practicing ideologues in *Washington*, but not in Lansing, or Columbus, or Springfield, or the other state capitals. I don't think many of you tuck yourselves in at night reading Adam Smith. Eighteenth Century economic theories don't help you explain to your constituents why the local steel mill is going belly-up.

"As governors, you've got to be pragmatic. You've got to *govern*. You've got to solve *problems—and you have to solve them today*."

Practice: Think of something that people in your organization may not want to hear but which you believe is important for them *to* hear. Write a paragraph in strong, simple language attempting to persuade them of the need to take action on this issue.

Like most leaders, Iacocca knows the power of words and their inextricable connection to persuasion and even to politics. He would no doubt agree with Pearl Strachan's caveat to "Handle words carefully, for words have more power than atom bombs."

In this chapter, we shall examine certain techniques leaders use to empower themselves and others by way of persuasive language. We will see how carefully words are handled by Tom Peters in an address to the National Press Club. We will examine his persuasive remarks from three perspectives: the definitions of leadership language provided by Cuomo, Iacocca, and Peters himself.

Defined by Peters

Tom Peters' response to the question, "What, in your opinion, constitutes the language of leadership?", echoes Vance Packard's suggestion that we must influence others to do what we believe is right. A certain amount of manipulation is implied in this definition, but manipulation is just what is needed if the leader is to persuade others to follow him.

Here, then, is Mr. Peters' response, which he entitled "Leaders and Symbols."

> "The essence of humanness is our language capability. A leader has only his or her language (the language of words *and* consistent, supporting deeds) as a 'tool.' To say that language is everything for the leader is not overstatement. It is fact.

> "Words, of course, are symbols. A leader's actions are symbolic. By his or her words (and deeds), he or she sets agendas, shows special concern for this topic and not that, and makes meaning and injects vigor or lethargy into an institution, be it a five-person accounting office or a nation. The leader, at any level, consciously considers himself or herself a manipulator (in the best sense) of symbols.

> "In particular, most effective leaders (again, at any level) are good storytellers. By that I don't necessarily mean artful raconteurs. I do mean that the tools/'symbols' they use most (on a day-to-day basis) is examples of others achieving things in the distant past or recent past.

> "How we do things 'around here' or 'the new way' are best illustrated, not by dry, lifeless policy proclamations or manuals, but feisty stories of peers doing this or that which illustrates in 'human language' that we can get from here to there. The good news is that story-telling can be learned, planned, and practiced. The 'trick,' of course, is having an exciting and worthy message in the first place, and then consistently reinforcing its outcroppings, day after day, year after year, without letup."

Practice: Write down a goal you believe you should strive to achieve, or a message you think is worthwhile for your organization. Now give examples of others achieving things to show how your organization can go from "here" (the current state of accomplishment) to "there" (the future state of accomplished goals).

In Chapter Three, we cited research which showed how much more persuasive stories are than statistics, just as Peters suggests. Before returning to the actual language of Tom Peters to see how it reflects the definitions of our three leaders, let us first consider some general guidelines for the use of persuasive language and the degrees of force that should be aligned with particular circumstances. What follows is the "Three-C" approach to using persuasion.

Compel

Different situations call for different persuasion tactics. There are times when you are completely in the right and so are in a superior position. By using the "compel" approach, you can use verbiage which is a little stronger, a little more assertive. By "compel," we mean you can afford to be a little less apologetic or explanatory. A compelling stance does not mean you would coerce or force others to your point of view. Rather, you can expedite the persuasion process since you have the advantage.

Compelling persuasive efforts can get to the point more readily, since less "build-up" time is required to develop a persuasive argument for the case being presented.

Concede

When we, as influencers, do not have the upper hand, so to speak, we must tread a little more softly. The "concede" tactics we would use in such circumstances might include flattery or praise or humility, depending upon the psychological needs of the individual we wish to persuade. The "concede" approach to persuasion works when you are not at an advantage and therefore expect to have to work harder to overcome resistance.

The "concede" strategy includes a careful development of one's position, an anticipation, and delicate rebuttal, of the target's likely opposition, and a convincing presentation of the benefits that would accrue to your targeted audience if you obtained what you were seeking. It may also include admitting that you were wrong in the past, or conceding the riskiness of your proposal, etc.

When you concede, you may have to admit a negative about yourself in order to obtain an ultimate positive.

Compromise

Often, our persuasive efforts are not conducted in an us-versus-them mood. When we are willing to make trade-offs, rather than be adversarial, the compromise approach works best. The use of logic and well-substantiated reasons will help us better bargain for our position. Compromise when neither you nor the other party stands to win *or* to lose a great deal. Use compromise when you need to discuss, not to deal.

Practice: Let's examine three memos, each of which reflects a different persuasive technique. As you read, fill in the word "compel," "concede," or "compromise" to describe the approach used to develop the persuasive memo. The writer of the memos wishes to take vacation during the first week in July, when his wife will also be on vacation.

Memo #1   As you know, Mr. Forrest, I have not taken my scheduled vacations for the past three years. You'll remember that we always seemed to have a crisis arise when it was time for me to take off. I willingly put the company's priorities above my own, especially because I had no particular plans to go anywhere. I was happy to take an occasional day off here and there to make up that vacation time.

This year, however, I *have* made plans. My wife will be taking the same two weeks off and we plan to go to Hawaii to celebrate our tenth wedding anniversary. I'm telling you well in advance so that—should another crisis arise—you can make plans to have someone else cover the situation.

APPROACH _____

Memo #2   I have been thinking about the vacation scheduling, Mr. Forrest, and I think I have found a way to make it equitable for everyone. If you have a half hour to spare, I'd like to go over my plan with you. I think it will ensure that everyone—including you and me—is able to take the days he or she is scheduled to take. If we can just have a reserve column of employees to cover for emergencies, then I think we can virtually guarantee equity in the vacation schedule. Let me show you what I've worked out.

APPROACH _____

Memo #3   Jon, remember when you were going through that burn-out period, when you had been working too hard and the stress was really getting to you? Then you went away for two weeks and somehow you found the key for coping with all these production problems. And when you came back, you looked and acted like a different man. It was as if 20 years had slipped away and you had a whole, new, youthful, invigorated approach to everything. Remember?

Well, I think I'm going through the same kind of stress-induced burnout right now. I need a vacation, Jon. I need to come back the way you came back—*in control*.

APPROACH _____

The first memo uses a *compel* style, since the influencer has the advantage. Knowing that he might encounter resistance from his boss, the author suggests that the boss might be violating certain organizational norms by calling upon him to deal with crises even when the author was supposed to be on vacation. He is also firmly stating that he is determined to leave this year, and that the boss should plan on having other employees deal with the fires that will probably need to be put out.

The *compromise* approach is evident in the second memo; we find the writer is using a professional, mature tone. He is not demanding. (Notice the use of the word "if".) He appears to be more concerned with organizational goals than personal benefit—the situation in which compromise works best.

The final memo clearly employs an emotional appeal in its *concede* approach. The writer is using flattery as well as a ploy for sympathy as he attempts to persuade the boss of the importance of a vacation. By reminding the boss of how the vacation revived the boss' flagging spirits, the writer is in essence implying that he deserves as much spirit-renewal as the boss.

Psychological Aspects

The leader in a given situation may or may not be in a superior position. But the leader knows how to use language in order to take control of the situation, knows how to persuade others to engage in ac-

The leader feels are worthwhile.

tivities that the leader feels are worthwhile. The leader also knows that the language of persuasion is imbued with psychological ramifications. In addition to deciding what tactical approach would work best for a specific set of circumstances, the leader also considers the choice of words, the possible effect of those words, and even the placement of those words in a conversation or memo.

Examine the following persuasive memos and decide which is most persuasive. Then go back and analyze the message presented in each. Encircle those sentences which are well-expressed and convincing. Underline those other sentences which will probably impair the writer's chance of eliciting approval from his superior.

Memo A   I would like to go to an Effective Decision-Making seminar which will be held the first week in March. The cost of the seminar is fairly high, but it should be worth it. I'll be happy to tell you everything I learned afterwards. I know that the first week in March will be a hectic one because we will have just submitted our budgets and will need to attend to all the work we didn't get done while we were working on them. However, the workshop is only being held once this year and that is in March. My secretary can handle most of my work, though, while I am away.

You know that I intend to move up in this organization and I will need to sharpen my decision-making skills so I can handle executive situations. This workshop will prepare me for future promotions. So, if you think the class is valuable, I hope you will sign this request.

Memo B   As you know, I have been looking for ways that I can gain some skill in dealing with the everyday problems that arise in my position. I think I have found a way to give me the decision-making skills that I lack. ABC University is holding a one-week seminar in early March; the focus is improving decision-making abilities. The cost is $1,500. I've checked around and learned that P.R. Septill, head of Purchasing, attended a similar seminar last year and found it valuable. I am certain I will find this one equally valuable if you will just grant me your permission to attend. I need the check voucher by the end of the week.

Memo C   When we met recently for my performance review, you expressed a concern about my ability to make decisions quickly and effectively. I agreed with your assessment and assured you that I would take steps to improve my skills in that area. Consequently, I was pleased to learn that ABC University will be presenting a workshop on that very topic, to be held the first week in March (an ideal time, since our budgets will have been completed by then). The workshop leader is Morton Stampley, whose book on that topic is currently on the Management Bestseller list.

Since the workshop will be held nearby, there will be no additional costs for lodging; I shall be happy to pay for my own meals. The only charge then will be for the workshop itself. And—to make that tuition fee of $1,500 cost-effective for the firm—I would be happy to share what I have learned with others, either in the form of a report on the proceedings or else in a brief presentation during the weekly staff meeting. Because the enrollment is limited, I would like to expedite the registration. If you approve this request, I will call ABC today to sign up.

Practice: Analyze the last persuasive memo you wrote. Which approach did you take? Was it the appropriate approach given the circumstances? In view of the preceding discussion, how might you alter your communication to make it more persuasive?

The Language of Words and Consistent Supporting Deeds

Tom Peters has fulfilled his own first requirement for a leader: to exemplify through words and actions the tenets to which he is committed. Through his books, his columns, his tapes, his appearances, his training programs, and his consulting activities, he has supported his beliefs regarding managerial excellence. The leader is one who *does* something about his concerns, who takes action to bring us closer to his vision of an improved state. There is no doubt of Peters' contribution to the excellence cause.

Practice: Do *your* actions reify your words? You may wish to verify the strength of your commitment by answering the following questions.

1. What do I believe about my organization? In what ways do I think it can be improved?

2. To whom and when have I expressed these beliefs?

3. What have I actually done to make that ameliorated vision a reality?

Setting a Positive Tone

To establish that initial rapport with an audience, to win them over so they will be more receptive to his remarks, the leader begins with a "concede" style.

Note the words of flattery, praise and even humility in Mr. Peters' opening remarks to the National Press Club. He uses them in this initial attempt to persuade others to his point of view.

Concede Approach

"I am deeply flattered and delighted to have been asked to speak to this august body. It's a great pleasure to be with you today."

"The words appeared somewhere in the middle [of the introduction of Peters to the audience] that 'He is clear in his mission.' My topic today is 'Confusion.'"

"One of the things that is confused is me."

While the tone of Peters' remarks alternates between "compel" and "compromise" through most of his presentation, we do find the "concede" approach emerging again during the question-and-answer period at the end of his speech. (As you read the following, pay attention to the many elements we have thus far discussed, including variety in sentence structure, variety in sentence length, humor, and the use of simple and direct language.)

Question: If we are involved in the destruction of hierarchy, why is merger mania persisting in this country at a faster and bigger pace than last year, six months after the crash was said to have killed mergers?

Peters' reply: I wish I could stand up here and rebut that with lots and lots of numbers. I can't. My own assessment of the situation is sort of two-fold. Obviously, big news is when two big things become something bigger. There is no news when demerging takes place. To my knowledge, and this was certainly true a couple of years ago, though I don't know what's happened since October of '87 to be honest with you, the dollars and the number of institutions involved in demerging, which doesn't make any headlines, were significantly greater than those that are involved with merging.

Mergers are driven by ego. I don't know why the hell we do it. The good news is we are a little less bad than we were and the Europeans are getting much worse. Since this is a competitive environment, maybe that's relatively good news.

Question: Long-term, won't the hierarchies still be around? What happens if everyone is a boutique?

Peters' reply: First of all, it's a little excessive to call Benetton a pre-teen market or else I'm a pre-teen female, because I have a wonderful, nice, rather adult-size cashmere sweater that came from one of Benetton's many experimental outlets.

There are two answers. First of all, the whole world is becoming boutiques: boutiques in semiconductors, boutiques in computers, boutiques in financial services, boutiques in retailing, boutiques in health care. I mean "boutiques" makes it sound like three people in a back room shop. Markets are fragmenting everywhere.

The Japanese are on this kick. The Japanese mass production strength is being gutted by the efficiency and excellence of the Koreans and the Taiwanese. And the Japanese within their sizable firms are now working on decentralization, independent business units, created so that they can play the higher value-added, niche-market game.

We find in the following response honesty, simplicity of expression, admission of his own fallibility, humor, directness, and emotion.

Question: Is it feasible to apply your decentralization ideas to government agencies from the State Department to Agriculture?

Peters' reply: State Department, I don't know. I think the answer is in general, clearly yes. Unfortunately, from the public sector standpoint...almost all the decentralization we have seen has been driven by external and competitive pressures in the private sector.

I'm terrified at the slowness with which our private sector giant firms are changing. My own sad observation is that people change when the gun is at their temple.

Question: Your own politics aside, does it appear that the White House is well-managed as a bureaucracy?

Peters' reply: That's a contradiction in terms, isn't it?

I was almost alone...in thinking that this new weapons czar, the Deputy Secretary for Weapons, was the stupidest idea I had ever heard of in my life.

Managing the White House is generally an impossible task. It probably hasn't been done very well since Abraham Lincoln was there. I've not applied myself intellectually to that task because I am not given to hopeless tasks.

Question: If tomorrow were Election Day, who would win and why?

Peters' reply: As to who would win tomorrow? It's got to be the world's most irrelevant question. And since I make so many mistakes myself, I am sympathetic. It's a better form of government than any other, but, my God, it disgusts me at times. I love the system, but it's a little absurd.

Compel Approach

In this address, Peters employs concede tactics in his initial attempts to establish concert with his listeners. At other times, however, his strategy involves a harder edge. In many respects, Peters had the advantage when he addressed the Press Club, enabling him to assume a strong posture.

He had a captive audience, for one thing; he was an invited guest, for another, a guest to whom the audience would accord respect. His was an international reputation. In short, he could well afford to take a hard line with some of the points he wanted to make, especially with points that contradicted prevalent thinking or that criticized some of the institutions Americans hold dear.

When he does contradict or criticize those institutions, he embodies Iacocca's definition of the leader as one who convinces others to believe things they may not want to believe.

Graphic words

The strength of Peters' message is captured in certain graphic words:

"exploded"..."sluggish"..."radical"..."bloody"..."economic disaster"

Hyperbole

His voice rings with authority as he incorporates hyperbole to lend force to his assertions.

"The absence of a trade bill still means that we have moved faster in the direction of protectionism in the last ten years than anybody else. It's a horrible bill. Not the plant-closing part of it. I think that's just...an attention-getter. The basic notion of that bill is restriction and this ain't the time.

"The only strength that we have (and this is my optimistic half) is we are moving faster than anybody else to restructure because the doors are open to competition and that has been the United States' strength in the last 300 years. Our open domestic market. And throughout our history we have in fact played by a stupid set of rules, according to some people, that looked altruistic. Not so.

"The main beneficiaries of radical decentralization in the United States have been the American consuming public, the citizenry. On the small business side of it, whatever we can do to enhance entrepreneurship. While I am certainly not in favor of reduced capital gains for growth of value in art work, I think that the capital gains reduction of the differential tax in the '86 tax bill should go down in history as one of the ten dumbest acts in the last 25 years—though there is a lot of competition for that particular accolade, I realize."

Other hyperbolic statements reinforce his position; they sharpen the pointed edge of his remarks even further:

"After all, it was only 25 years ago when Ken Olsen was the only guy on the planet who believed in decentralized computation."

"The level of smog [in certain industrial cities of China] is such that California, or L.A., rather, on its bad days looks like paradise by comparison."

"Fred Smith gives the Postmaster General indigestion."

"There is an entrepreneurial spurt in this country which is not only unmatched around the globe but which is the envy of the globe including Japan."

"The Limited or Benetton can restock and change what they are doing in their stores five or ten or fifteen or twenty times faster than a Sears or J.C. Penney's or any of the traditional retailers."

"We see it at least anecdotally, and I think the anecdotal seeing is more important than ever. By the time it shows up in the regression equations, we'll all be dead."

Authoritative tone

Aware of the discomfort with which most people view change, Peters nonetheless insists on the need for change. He comes on strong, so to speak, to startle his listeners into recognizing the need to alter the status quo.

"Only the persuaded can persuade," it has been observed. There is little doubt that Mr. Peters has been persuaded of the need for change. And he uses less than gentle persuasion to demonstrate to his audience the seriousness of his message. The definitive statements which follow resonate with authority. (Look for the parallel structure which lends a rhythmic logic to the words.)

"Big firms exist in a predictable world. Big firms, giant ones— I'm not talking tiny ones; I'm not talking mom-and-pop grocery stores here—giant firms have a difficult time existing when there is total uncertainty. The basic premise behind hierarchy and size is one word: predictability.

"You get rid of predictability and you have destroyed the basic premise for human organization in the basic sense that we regularly know it.

"I will tell you exactly what I think needs to happen.

"I think that our big firms have a lot to do. Our big firms must become obsessed with quality rather than mass. Our big firms must become obsessed with product design which they are not now. Our big firms must become obsessed with the creation of niche markets, rather than mass markets."

Not one to succumb to buzz words which so quickly lose their impact, Peters supplies some definitions of his own in his typical no-nonsense style.

Definitions

"The employee must become the principal source of value added. That means an awesome commitment to—not training—I *hate* that word 'training,' but continuous learning for every employee, for every day of his or her career.

"In the same vein, I don't like this word 'empowerment' that we're using a lot in business, either, because that's kind of been bastardized in the last year or so.

"Not empowerment, let's call it straight. Giving away power. You can't move 15 times faster than the other guy unless the person close to the front has the information and the authority and the power to decide. Period."

Practice: Reflect on some persuasive communication you will have to prepare in the near future. Select a situation which requires you to assert your authority by using a "compelling" strategy. It may be, for example, that you are about to introduce some procedural or systematic change which you know will be resisted by your subordinates. Prepare a communication that exemplifies a forceful stance through graphic words, hyperbole, a serious message, an authoritative tone, and/or new definitions.

Compromise Approach

Most often, however, Peters draws on compromise tactics to persuade others of his concerns about America's economy, and to convince them of the correctness of his views.

When a persuader seeks a cooperative spirit, when he has attacked and then withdrawn, when he has so alarmed his audience that they are ready to work toward a solution, the leader then deploys a rational strategy. At this point, resistance is no longer an issue; rather the persuader is hoping to inspire others to work toward a common goal.

In the following passage, we find Peters shaping a plan of action for his listeners (including the television audience) by telling what must be done: American business must model itself after firms (described as follows) that have achieved success.

Specific examples

"They are getting rid of businesses that don't fit...."

"They are savagely reducing hierarchy, often by 50 or 75%."

"They are establishing many, many more highly autonomous business units."

"They are radically reducing factory size."

"They are enhancing the role of small, autonomous business units, creating factories within factories."

"They are using more and more and more subcontractors."

"They are turning to smaller and more coherent multi-functional teams to develop their businesses."

"They are linking incentives to small unit performance."

"They are beginning to emphasize small markets, niche markets, higher value-added products."

Optimism

The use of "we" in the following reflects Peters' faith in the national efforts under way. He catalogs those efforts, thereby providing a specific rationale for his optimism.

> "We are in the midst of a new form of human organization that will be required to compete in any market in the world. We are in the era of destruction of hierarchy—not reduction. We have all these pabulum words...flattening the hierarchy, becoming a little more fleet of foot...we're destroying hierarchy."

> "The reason I think is fairly obvious: roughly speaking, Honda can develop a car five or six times faster than GM or even Ford. In the same vein, Compaq can develop a new computer three or four or five times faster than IBM."

Practice: Reflect on some persuasive communication you will have to prepare in the near future. Select a situation that calls for a compromise approach, i.e., neither you nor your audience has a distinct advantage. In such circumstances, resistance is usually not an issue. Instead, while the influencer may wish to obtain benefits for herself, she is also concerned about the larger unit, be it a company or a country.

Keep in mind Peters' compromise strategy as you write: the inclusion of specific facts and examples to substantiate points, a cooperative spirit, optimism, a sense of "can-do," and the seeking of the greatest good for the greatest number.

Leadership Language

Tom Peters' words display so many of the aspects of leadership language discussed in the first two chapters that we will cite only a few examples here.

Metaphor

"The trade balance is looking better, but only because we have become the Argentina of North America in terms of our currency."

"Someone in the press...referred to me at one point as the 'Dr. Feelgood of Management.'"

Alliteration

"mega-merger mania"

Opinionated statement

"Service and low-tech do not go together as a general proposition."

"The budget situation is disgusting. The debt situation is worse."

"Given the last 2000 years of organizing, 'fast' and 'traditional organization' do not belong in the same sentence."

"My own supposition is that we are in the midst of the most significant structural change in the way business is organized and executed...in the last 2000 years."

"It's the American penchant for overcomplexity."

Personification

Peters treats the abstract concept of a corporation as if it were a person suffering from a physical malady or physical violence.

"We have just become, hopelessly in some respects, constipated in our giant firms."

"IBM at some level is being murdered."

Questions

Peppered throughout Tom Peters' remarks are questions designed to challenge, to mentally provoke his listeners:

"What are the big companies doing?"

"Why are there two radically different points of view?"

"What has Sears done?"

"And, where, by the way, did the chairman of IBM go to get advice on how to reorganize his $50 billion dollar company?"

Anecdote

As we have learned, Peters believes that "most effective leaders are good storytellers." He began his delivery to the Press Club with the story of a recent visit:

"I had the privilege to spend about five weeks lecturing and observing over there [The People's Republic of China]. In fact, that visit provides a metaphor in some respects for this talk itself. Many have written and discussed the fact that there are two Chinas. I don't think there is a bit of hyperbole in that description whatsoever."

Additional components of leadership language

There are other aspects of leadership language which are manifest in the words of Tom Peters. For example, when he is enthusiastic about a company or a concept, he makes no attempt to disguise or qualify his zeal.

Unbridled praise

We can virtually hear the glee in his voice as he asserts,

"The start-ups are going gangbusters."

"Ted Turner has, to put it mildly, surprised a few people at the three networks in the last half-dozen years."

"The Limited Stores are a high-tech marvel."

"It's what I call America's twenty most important companies. The importance of the list...is there couldn't be any country in the world where such a list could be developed.

"No country could generate a list that touches that. Germany couldn't generate a list that was one-fifth that long of interesting firms."

"Since Honda and SONY, Japan could not generate any sizable start-ups of that sort and it's the major problem that they face."

"...I don't know whether the excitement that the list brings out in me describes the new world."

"The one thing for sure is that it is going to be a very exciting few years."

How can one help but be caught up in the fervor, the force of such a promise? Peters knows that you must be committed to an issue if you expect others to be committed as well. His willingness to spread the optimistic word helps us believe in him and in the possibilities he describes.

Practice: 1. What are some aspects of your firm or industry for which you feel considerable excitement? Let your enthusiasm show through as you write about those ideas or possibilities or happenings that create a fire, so to speak, within you. Now, explain how you can take a leadership stance which would involve sharing your excitement with others. When and where and how would that sharing occur?

2. Can you think of a promise that you might make about your own efforts (or those of your department or firm) and the future payoff that will be the result of those efforts? You need not make your promise public, but you should put it in writing and list dates for expected achievement.

Common words

Peters' words are eager, unrestrained, dynamic—much like the man himself. He achieves this verbal vitality, in part, because he uses the common language that Iacocca so admires. No sesquipedalian terms here. Just listen to the appeal of these clear and powerful words—devoid of the verbal inflation so often found within the corporate realm.

"Since I was not able to muster anything of intelligence in the way of an intellectual argument, I decided to do the cop-out route and just write a list down. List season is about over so I get mine now."

"There is a case for that [restructuring]. I wouldn't guarantee it, but it's not silly. And if you are not moving as fast—as a business person—as that change suggests, you are probably in serious trouble."

"GM is screwing it up. The Limited is doing it well. Why? The Limited has applied technology in the context of a hierarchy-less organization. GM is using the new technology with the same old 29 ½ layered structure."

"The big-firm message to me...is one key word and that word is 'flexibility.'"

Of course, the use of common language is not always admirable. Sometimes, it leads to uncommon expressions, such as these from movie maven Samuel Goldwyn:

"Let's have some new clichés."

"A verbal contract isn't worth the paper it's written on."

"I'll give you a definite maybe."

"I had a great idea this morning but I didn't like it."

"I'm going to have a bust made of my wife's hands."

"Anyone who goes to a psychiatrist should have his head examined."

"The only trouble with this business is the dearth of bad pictures."

Or these from Casey Stengel:

"Now all you fellows line up alphabetically by height."

"Now, there's three things you can do in a baseball game. You can win, or you can lose or it can rain."

Janusian Thinking

There are those who believe that the only way to come to grips with a problem is to consider it from two opposing points of view:

(1) the "thesis," which is the situation at hand, the supposition or hypothesis on which your course of action will be predicated and

(2) the "antithesis," or complete opposite of that stance, as wild or unthinkable as it might be.

This sort of thinking is termed Janusian, after the Roman god Janus. The month of January is derived from his name. Janus was depicted on Roman coins with two faces: one looking toward the year that had just ended and the other looking in the opposite direction, toward the year that was about to begin.

Janusian thinking is the most simplistic definition of Hegelian dialectics: the thesis is combined with the antithesis to derive the synthesis or workable course of action. We find Peters repeatedly expressing himself in Janusian terms. Here is the description of an "intellectual journey of the last nine or ten years," a piece he was asked to write for *Inc.* magazine.

"Some colleagues...suggested that the idea, from their observation, was that it be titled 'From Optimism to Cynicism and Back Again.'"

Again, at the very beginning of his remarks, he admits

"Were you to have the patience and we to have the time, I think I could give two radically different speeches today. I think that I could give you a stem-winding, analytically sound, logically coherent data-based speech on the fact that America...is going (or has gone) to hell in a handbasket.

"I think I could give you an equally well-argued and data-based speech that says America has adapted to the structural changes that are clearly going on in the world, better than anyone else so far, including the Japanese, even though there are a lot of numbers that don't make many of us happy at this stage of the game.

"The problem is I don't have any idea which one of those speeches is the right one."

Peters clearly feels comfortable with paradoxes; in fact, one of the descriptions he likes to use about himself is that he is "thriving on chaos," a term he has chosen for the title of his recent book. He confesses further:

"I don't have any idea of what is going on, but I genuinely feel comfortable in the set of prescriptions that are required to get us out of whatever it is that we are in the middle of."

He assures his audience that

"There is an answer to this confusion."

but continues to ask,

"Why are there two radically different points of view?"

Practice: Fully describe a conflict or a problem facing your firm or your industry. (If you wish to think in more global terms, describe some of the issues with which American business must grapple in the coming years.) Try to state the problem from two opposing points of view (the thesis and the antithesis) and then attempt to resolve these differing perspectives into a workable solution or synthesis.

Rice's View

In a speech delivered at the Annual Convocation of the National Junior Classical League at Indiana University, George P. Rice, Professor of Rhetoric and Public Speaking at Butler University, made a number of points which underscore the emphases of this book. In bringing the classical perspective to bear on the contemporary communicator,

Rice raises some of the same issues that our identified leaders have addressed. He begins with a discussion of style:

> The Roman rhetorician Seneca said that "...style is the man himself." Let us agree that the essence of style is found in two qualities: the ideas one wishes to present, and the selection and arrangement of the words used to convey these ideas.[18]

These are the very qualities on which we have focused in this book: the content and the context of leadership language. In his examination, Rice reviews the techniques used by ancient leaders such as Pericles, Cicero, and Caesar. Rice asks if those techniques are applicable to modern needs and then asserts they are.

Analyzing governing bodies from which great orators arose, Rice notes that those bodies protected freedom of speech and encouraged oratory on issues that were often controversial. The eloquent leaders of the past were men of integrity, a trait that we have repeatedly stressed as being integral to leadership.

Rice does not feel these conditions for fostering freedom existed in Hitlerian Germany nor in Communist countries. As a result, leaders in those polities did not exemplify leadership language, as they did not invest their leadership with the moral responsibility required for those who respect and permit freedom.

Among the requirements for leadership language are the following paraphrased features. Based in antiquity, Rice tells us, they are nonetheless applicable to the present.

1. Speeches should have a beginning, middle and end.
2. Each part of the speech has a specific purpose.
3. The four aspects of all communications are the speaker, the speech, the audience, and the occasion.
4. The good communicator will observe the rules of grammar and syntax.
5. The components of persuasive communication include moral, logical and emotional choices.

6. When dealing with emotional issues, definitions must be used, and the pairing of opposites [Janusian thinking] as well. The speech should be "sealed with a final calm."

7. Argumentation requires the evidence to support it.

8. The effective persuader relies upon example, generalization, quotation, precedent, definition, analogy, etc.

9. The aim of oratory is its effect, rather than permanence or elegance.[19]

Practice: Utilize the following classical guidelines the next time you have an important presentation to deliver. (The first three pertain to your written communications as well as the spoken.)

1. **inventio**   Gather the material you will need.

2. **dispositio**   Arrange it in the body of the speech.

3. **electuio**   Select the style that is appropriate for the speaker, audience, subject, and occasion.

4. **memoria**   Commit to memory the basic ingredients of speech, in the proper order.

5. **actio**   Make use of voice, gestures, and bodily movements to make the speech more memorable for your audience.[20]

Conclusion

Rice concludes his speech, as we will this chapter, with five recommendations that transcend the centuries to bring direction to leaders seeking to use language in the most persuasive way possible. These recommended elements of style serve as a comprehensive summary of the specific points made in this chapter.

1. The speaker or writer must be endowed with creative imagination of a high level of insight.

2. His creative drive must be sustained by strong emotion from beginning to end of his composition.
3. He must exhibit able command of metaphor and other figures of speech.
4. He must have good diction, an excellent vocabulary and be able to use it.
5. The structuring of the piece should exhibit awareness of order.[21]

The next section of the book deals with the leadership language of notable figures from the worlds of psychology, journalism, social science and entertainment. We shall explore the language that has helped to propel these figures into leadership positions in their respective communities.

CHECKLIST

☐ Have I followed the five classical steps in the preparation of this communication?

☐ Have I applied Janusian thinking to an issue of common concern in order to resolve it?

☐ Have I evaluated the persuasive situation to determine if a "compel," "concede," or "compromise" position should be taken?

☐ Will the audience appreciate a humorous tone in this communication?

☐ Might the audience be offended by certain words or descriptions? If so, have I omitted those references?

☐ Knowing what aspects of our (corporate) culture are important to my reader, have I tried to emphasize those aspects?

☐ Have I placed negative or unwelcome information in a strategic location?

☐ Have I led up to that information, rather than springing it on my audience?

☐ Have I wasted their time with unimportant information?

☐ Have I focused on the advantages that might ensue if this plan is adopted?

☐ Have I anticipated likely objections and overcome them with the force of my persuasive argument?

☐ Are there precedents I can cite to strengthen my position?

☐ Have I substantiated the force of my persuasion with supportive data?

Footnotes

[16] Bennis, op. cit., p. 33.

[17] From *Diaries of Mario M. Cuomo* by Mario M. Cuomo (New York: Random House, 1984), p. 115. Reprinted by permission of Random House, Inc.

[18] George P. Rice, "Classical Theories of Communication," *Vital Speeches of the Day,* October 1, 1986, Vol. LII, No. 214, p. 763. Reprinted with permission.

[19] Ibid., p. 764.

[20] Ibid., p. 765.

[21] Ibid., p. 764.

CHAPTER FIVE:
The Language of Psychology: A Study of Judith Bardwick's Words

> *One of the most serious problems confronting psychology is that of connecting itself with life.... Theory that does not some way affect life has no value.*
> Lewis Madison Terman

Introduction

As every study of leadership will assert, the leader must be one who has a vision: a vision that of necessity encompasses and embraces change. To be able to articulate that future-oriented ideal requires considerable thought and research and exchanging of ideas.

Dr. Judith Bardwick is one who has expended the necessary effort toward developing an expressible concern about the future. She has published more than 60 journal articles and book chapters on current issues, and has authored *The Plateauing Trap, The Psychology of Women, In Transition,* and *Earn It: From Entitlement to Earning.* Her psychological contributions have value precisely because they do connect to life; she has gone beyond theory to have an impact on the lives of her readers.

Before turning to her assessment of future workplace concerns, let us examine what others have had to say about futuristic issues.

Significant Challenges

In its 95th anniversary issue, *Business Month* asked, "What is the most significant challenge American business faces?"[22] Here are the responses from some of America's most articulate leaders.

Zane E. Barnes, Chairman and CEO, Southwestern Bell:
"Educating employees to provide tomorrow's high-tech services and products. The corporate fight for a competitive edge will be decided in our schools."

Paul A. Bilzerian, Chairman and CEO, Singer:
"To be more responsive to the needs of two constituencies that are crucial to every company's success—its shareholders and its work force."

William W. Boeschenstein, President, Chairman and CEO, Owens-Corning Fiberglas:
"Negotiating a mine field of shifting attitudes and statutes in the regulatory environment. The inability of equity markets is disrupting the partnership between investment and corporate development."

Frank V. Cahouet, Chairman and CEO, Mellon Bank:
"Becoming more adept at managing effectively in today's environment of accelerating change. Business leaders must be willing to shed traditional approaches and be more flexible."

Lee A. Iacocca, Chairman and CEO, Chrysler:
"Business, government and labor have to form a new partnership rooted in a 'will to compete' attitude, formalized in national economic policies that allow that will to result in a more competitive America. We need to rid ourselves of the crushing debt load, and we must insure that the great American market does not become the dumping ground for the world's excess industrial capacity. It's not American business that must learn to compete, but America itself."

Practice: In your own words, respond to the same question asked of these leaders, "What is the most significant challenge American business faces?"

The Power Factor

Like others concerned about the impact of trends upon the future of America's economy, Bardwick has her own agenda. Recognizing that in this pyramid-flattening era, there will be fewer and fewer promotional opportunities for an increasing number of promotables, she has done extensive writing and speaking about "plateauing," which she defines as "promotions ending long before retirement for most people."

Entitled "Pushing Power Down," the speech we are about to analyze mixes an understanding of power, the elements of persuasion, and the psychological insights she no doubt acquired from many years as a psychology professor at the University of Michigan.

Her words often parallel those of Roberto Goizueta, CEO of the Coca-Cola Company, who noted, "My university degree and my background are in chemical engineering. But over 90% of my time during my business career has been spent in dealing with people, understanding people, motivating people, appealing to people, and finally, trying to unite people in pursuit of our goals."

The Familiar Foundation

Bardwick begins with a reassuring, familiar point of view: the promotional process as most people understand it.

"In our very recent history, from 1950 to 1975, we experienced the greatest expansion in the size of our institutions we ever had. And the number of educated people, the number of qualified candidates for management, was small. As a result, those who were able, were promoted."

Practice: Describe the current and prevalent thinking, the familiar foundation on which the challenge you identified in the previous practice is based.

Cognitive Dissonance

Leon Festinger coined the phrase "cognitive dissonance" to explain the psychological discomfort we experience when we learn something that is upsetting to our intellectual/emotional balance. For example, what if you learned that someone you greatly admired—your minister, perhaps, or your child's teacher—had been arrested for drug possession? The news would be so disturbing that you would have to do something to resolve the dissonance you were feeling—that disruption that occurs when a basic belief is shattered.

To restore consonance, to re-establish equilibrium, you could do any number of things, but you would have to do something to restore balance to the beliefs that are now at odds with one another in your head.

You could tell yourself that it must be a case of mistaken identify. Or you could attempt to assuage the severity of the situation by telling yourself it was probably just a little bit of relatively harmless marijuana. Or you could completely reverse your opinion of the person, but you could not continue to hold in juxtaposition these two disparate views—of a respected member of the community and of a drug user.

We find Bardwick beginning the persuasive effort of leading her audience to a new belief by referring at first to the familiar, to the known, to the traditional. She evinces her understanding of motivation by using common elements of leadership language: she weaves psychological threads into the fabric of her persuasion. She has gained her audience's interest and acceptance by dealing with currently frozen attitudes before beginning the thawing process which she knows will cause some cognitive dissonance.

She introduces the first step of her recommendations for change by explaining the paradoxical need:

"But now we have the opposite conditions; we have the very largest number of educated people we have ever had, and the number of management positions is declining."

Corporations and individuals must begin to make accommodations for this paradox; otherwise, she assures us, productivity and work satisfaction will inevitably decline.

Supportive Data

To reinforce the importance of the changes the leader deems necessary, proof must be presented. In this case, that proof is in the form of demographic projections for the future.

"In 1950, 31% of American women were in the labor force. today, it's 76% and by 1995 it will be 80%.

"In 1960, 56 schools granted the MBA to 4,643 people. In 1986, 650 schools graduated 71,000 MBA's. Today, 200,000 students are studying for an MBA.

"From 1980 – 1990, the number of jobs in the professions and in management increased by 21%. The number of candidates went up by 42%.

"From 1986 to 1990, the number of jobs in middle management increased by 1.7 million. But the number of candidates grew to 10.4 million."

Practice: Imagine you are giving a speech on the challenge you identified earlier. What words and/or statistics would you as a leader use to persuade others to change their thinking?

The Rule of 99

To lend further credence to the importance of her view, to persuade her audience to align their thinking with hers, Bardwick asserts "The Rule of 99."

"We might say that people who reach the executive level, by definition, are not plateaued. How many people will get that high? In every large organization, we find the number of executive positions is always less than one percent of the number of employees. I call that "The Rule of 99." The structure of the organization creates a reality in which 99+ percent of employees will *not* reach the executive level. What percent of employees must, therefore, plateau? The answer is obvious: 99+ percent."

Soften a Harsh Reality

The psychologist in Bardwick is sensitive to the effect such an observation will have on the mass of [wo]men who do not wish to lead lives of quiet desperation. And so, she offers hope to them in the form of a new perspective. She invites the listener to rethink the meaning of "plateau."

"Today's plateauing problem is the opposite of the Peter Principle. People are not rising to their level of incompetence. Instead, the glut of candidates for promotion at a time when positions are shrinking results in many people not having an opportunity to reach levels of responsibility which they are perfectly able to manage. Today's plateauing has no relationship with failure. It is, instead, strictly a matter of those numbers."

She asserts,

"Being plateaued has to be transformed from a problem to an opportunity."

And later, in an equally assertive tone, she restates,

"Being plateaued has to become an honorable state."

For the remainder of her presentation, Bardwick exhorts leaders to help in this transformation of values so that the new thinking about plateauing can become a recognized feature of the corporate culture.

Offer Solutions

Having tackled a tough situation, she is now prepared to offer some welcome advice. And that, of course, is the leader's role: not only to identify the problems—current and future—but also to offer workable solutions. (This view parallels what Governor Cuomo said earlier; he deemed it political suicide to identify problems and not offer solutions.) As she maintains, there is hope when there is a sense of something being done, whether it's for the organization as a whole or for the individuals within that organization:

> "Institutions are plateaued when there's no sense of momentum, and individuals feel plateaued when they feel stuck. Thus, plateaued organizations and individuals have no clear sense of a future because there's no feeling of movement toward anything. *The task for the organization, its mangers, and for individual employees, is to face the issue of disappointment and then go beyond that, creating a future by creating new goals that emphasize the excitement of challenge."*

Reassure

The leader knows that followers sometimes need the reassurance of her words to encourage them that a project they are being urged to undertake can succeed. Persuasive and psychological aspects of leadership language are entwined; we find evidence of them both in the following excerpt. The difficulty of the task is acknowledged, to be sure, but encouragement is provided in the mention of the time it will take to institute this new way of thinking. The leader does not expect new attitudes to be developed overnight.

> "While it's realistically difficult to achieve fundamental changes in complex institutions, in a sense all of this is very simple. The message to organizations is this: *You have to increase the number of categories of contributing, or the types of career paths, which people can experience as successful. You cannot restrict esteem to the fewer and fewer who will be climbing up the management ladder. You need to have the majority of your people feeling like winners."*

Practice: Acquire information about trends that will impact your company or industry in the near future. Then use that information in a message to colleagues. The tone of your message should be authoritative, as Bardwick's is in the preceding passage, but it should also be encouraging. Offer a clear and accomplishable solution.

Kaye's View

In *Up Is Not the Only Way: A Guide for Career Development Practitioners,* Beverly Kaye echoes Bardwick's exhortation about the need to make people feel like winners through creative reward options:

> Most current organizational reward systems rely on techniques that have been used for a considerable time, such as bonus pay, employee-of-the-month recognition, extra leave or vacation time, and an occasional pat on the back. Thinking beyond these, practitioners can expand the options into new and more experimental strategies that have only recently come into use.

Kaye suggests cafeteria-style benefits packages, in which employees choose how benefits will be selected. Job enrichment is another option, for it permits decision-making involvement and control over tasks. Greater self-determination in performance feedback and alternative work patterns are additional possibilities. Such rewards, claims Kaye,

> are particularly relevant to those employees whose career development does not lead to vertical moves and perhaps not even to horizontal moves. Even without movement to another job, the career development participants must receive clear signals from the organization that their learning and growth is recognized and valued.[23]

Repeat Your Message

The more important the message, the greater the need for an audience to be reminded of it. Bardwick repeats her basic theme, bringing a new emphasis each time. She talks about her vision: she really does "see" the change in thinking coming about, but she admits it will be difficult. Fundamental shifts in the psychological terrain take time.

But those changes in values will occur simply because people need to feel successful. Reality will cause the majority to broaden their concept of success. But it will take time and it will take work because changing the concept of success involves very basic psychological change.

Turn a Negative into a Positive

Leaders anticipate change and offer ways to make the change process less threatening. The world of work was once a predictable world. People were hired, employed, retired—by the same company. Their employment included rewards in the form of pay increases and promotions for work done well. Employees could expect to be advanced and to be secure.

That world, however, no longer exists. Events have changed it dramatically. Downsizing, reorganization, takeovers, buy-outs, mergers, restructuring, pyramid-flattening—all of these have impacted employees who used to regard their companies as womb-to-tomb institutions. The rapidity with which the institutions are being altered has left many people confused, if not downright fearful. Not only are they no longer guaranteed of a promotion, they may not even be guaranteed of a job.

We hear Bardwick's voice—the voice of the psychologist—coming forth as the rational change-agent, calming people, but also encouraging them to accept the circumstances that have been imposed. Bardwick discusses optimum anxiety; she expresses the view (as do both Iacocca and Peters) that too much comfort and too little change may actually be counterproductive for a nation such as ours.

"In this period of turbulence there is an awful ending of some certainties and assumptions. We have: the end of job security for managers, executives and professionals; the end of certainty about the organization's and one's own future; and the early end of promotion for many.

"Those *ends* must be accepted as ends—and they must also be converted to *beginnings*. Surprisingly, those 'ends' are also windows for striking opportunities. A good way to think about this is in terms of the anxiety curve. Too little anxiety is as destructive to creative productivity as too much anxiety. In many corporations, notably the largest and most famous, in most governments and universities, and perhaps in our society as a whole, we got so secure that we got complacent. Smug."

Practice: Bardwick—with the "turnaround" idea of treating ends as beginnings—gives her audience an easily remembered phrase, a provocative expression which prompts further thought. Consider these other turnaround phrases and then work to come up with at least five of your own easily recalled sayings which can be used to express your business philosophy:

> "Our gifts are burdens: our burdens are gifts."

> "You do not stop because you grow old; you grow old because you stop."

> "America did not invent human rights; human rights invented America."
>
>   Jimmy Carter

> "When the going gets tough, the tough get going."

> "If you vote for the lesser of two evils, you get the evil of two lessers."

> "He is not a crisis manager; he is a crisis that has to be managed."

> "The Golden Rule: Those who have the gold, rule."

The Challenge Factor

The leader manages to inspire by admitting the existence of a problem and then presenting that problem as a challenge, replete with opportunities for growth and variety. Bardwick recognizes that the familiar world of "Work-hard-and-you-will-be-taken-care-of" is crumbling and that the new employment world is an uncertain one. She exhorts her listeners to be progressive in their thinking, to regard this unstable period of no guarantees as a time for making an imprint on the corporate quicksand by defining a goal.

What follows is her prescription for success.

"Thus, plateaued organizations and individuals have no clear sense of a future because there's no feeling of movement toward anything. The task for the organization, its managers, and for individual employees, is to face the issue of disappointment and then go beyond that, creating a future by creating new goals that emphasize the excitement of challenge. Facing and mastering a new task is engrossing. Full-out striving toward a goal is moving toward a future. That experience is optimistic; it is high-energy.

"And that outcome is achievable. The first task is to get out of the plateauing trap by facing the issues. The second is to create new goals."

Foreign competition, trade deficits, the collapse of the growth curve in some high-tech industries, divestiture, deregulation—so many factors are responsible for this period of transition in which corporations are viewed less and less as paternal protectors and individuals are viewed more and more as fend-for-yourselfers. Permanence has been replaced by flexibility, both in terms of thinking and in the nature of the work force.

While Bardwick insists we must change our mindsets to reflect the streamlining associated with corporate delayering (which Peters advocated in the preceding chapter), she nonetheless acknowledges the staying power of old values.

"Today we are in a transition period where old values of who is a winner co-exist with the new reality that there are fewer of those people. It is predictable that during the transition phase the old concepts are more powerful than the new values because the new values have a very short history. We didn't grow up with them."

Practice: Assume that you are head of a corporation which has undergone restructuring. Because of layoffs, the remaining employees are understandably concerned about their own future. What can you say to reassure them? You must acknowledge the possibility of further cutbacks, and yet you want their commitment and morale to remain high.

The Risk-Taking Factor

Mitchell Posner, writing in *Executive Essentials,* proposes that successful executives thrive on surmounting difficulties; they bask in the sense of achievement that can only be derived from meeting a challenge head-on and grappling with it to the end.

This description can probably be applied to anyone—executive or supervisor or clerk—who is interested in moving his or her career forward. Meeting challenges invariably involves risk-taking; the individual preoccupied with security (which is no longer as secure as it once was) is unlikely to go out on a limb, and equally unlikely to advance his or her career.

"Every executive must place himself [or herself] at risk in order to advance," insists Posner. Here are his guidelines for optimizing your risk-taking efforts.[24]

1. Never risk more than you can afford to lose.

2. Don't discount intuition.

3. Confront the fears that may be holding you back.

4. Know your limitations.

5. Always have a clear idea of how much authority you have and how much power you yield.

6. Know the rules.

7. Have a contingency plan.

8. Pay attention to time and place.

9. Gauge in advance just how far you can go.

10. Go for maximum impact.

11. Give 'em some space.

12. Know when to quit.

13. Judge your winnings and losses over the long term.

When Iacocca spoke of the leader as one who sets out to accomplish what others may not want to do, he also alluded to challenges, to the accomplishment of formidable tasks, such as turning Chrysler Corporation from a losing proposition to a thriving company once again. Lesser jobs require the same kind of spirit, which means abandoning security and moving along uncharted paths as necessary.

Here is what Bardwick has to say about corporate risk-taking:

"As I consult in some of our largest organizations, I see that the current increase in anxiety is not altogether bad news. That's because I see styles of behaving in those institutions that reflect a long history of an excess of security, of too little accountability, of too little anxiety."

Proper Perspective

The leader is often he who can put things in their proper perspective, he who does not succumb to prevalent buzz words but who instead examines the actual meaning of those words and their connotations. In a stress-conscious era, Bardwick actually challenges the negative stereotypes about pressure by pointing out that the total absence of stress may do individuals and organizations more harm than good.

"It seems to me that, over time, those organizations lost the cutting edge of drive, of innovation, of that mood of "Go for it!" Too secure, the institutions became ever more bureaucratic and the employees became systems players.

"When people in organizations feel too secure, it's because there aren't any significant outcomes as a result of what they do. Whatever you do, nothing much different happens. This also means there are no important pay-offs if you risk by innovating. As there are no rewards for taking risks, then there's no sense of **push** in that institution's culture."

The Confidence Factor

If you think about those people whom you regard as leaders, chances are that one of the traits you could identify in them is their self-confidence, the certitude with which they approach their goals, their unflappable conviction that what they are doing is the right thing to do and can be done. Leadership language smacks of faith.

The only way to acquire confidence, Bardwick asserts, is to

"...take risks, be accountable for the results, and have more successes than failures. Unless you've experienced some setbacks, some 'failures,' and worked past them, then you don't learn not to be afraid of 'failing.' Without experiences of being accountable, of taking risks, of winning and sometimes of losing, people are too afraid of taking risks."

"Experience," Oscar Wilde pointed out, "is the name everyone gives to their mistakes." We need this experience to succeed.

Definitions

As we have mentioned, in order to persuade others to follow her point of view, the leader must define her terms. In her efforts to defrost frozen attitudes about security, Bardwick explores both the connotative and the denotative aspects of it. And while union loyalists might disagree with her assertions, those who are primarily interested in progress and productivity and bottom-line results would probably agree. As you read Bardwick's definition, determine how many of the descriptions apply to your work unit.

"Whether in terms of an institution or an individual, if there's a lot of anxiety about risks, then the core motive is to gain security. 'Security' means avoiding failure. That becomes more important than achieving major breakthroughs. Over time, the culture and practices and procedures all develop in ways that unconsciously are designed to avoid failure. That includes:

- Informal tenure for everyone so it's very hard to fire the unproductive.
- An appraisal system without teeth.
- No negative feedback.
- A promotion system independent of individual merit.
- A culture in which competition is prohibited.
- A compensation system that doesn't reflect what people do.
- Fixed rules to determine what's right or wrong.
- Committees without authority to decide what's good or bad.
- A style of consensus but no disagreement is allowed.
- Rewarding systems players because initiators are scary.
- Leaders who are very conservative.
- Layers and layers of people whose primary job is to check and recheck to make sure that no mistakes can be made."

The Critical Factor

Tom Peters rails against the multi-layered organization, which he views as inefficient. Bardwick also rails, but she criticizes in an effort to loosen the security-tentacles.

"Institutions which have too much security thus tend to become bureaucratic. They add layers of people and layers of rules in order to assure the security of not making mistakes."

Practice: "Rail against" (or at least express your viewpoint about) some practice or belief in your company or industry that you feel is counter-productive. Make a list, as Bardwick does, of the many manifestations of that practice or belief.

Like Peters and Iacocca, Bardwick does not hesitate to criticize those traditions and institutions which—having scrutinized—she believes need reform.

"I am impressed and distressed at how passive hierarchical organizations make people. There's often a lot of overt activity, but it's not going anywhere, it's game-playing. It's play-acting at work."

As a leader, she employs language which challenges, which slaughters sacred cows, so to speak, in order that a psychological sustenance can be offered instead.

"Essentially, it's a situation in which there's a large core of powerlessness which is balanced against the unwritten contract that says that if you behave, you'll be okay. No wonder people pay so much attention to knowing the rules, to knowing the right people, to not making waves, to never making errors—to not risking, trying, innovating."

The Hope Factor

The leader offers alternatives. And, in this situation, Bardwick maintains the alternative is one of dynamic occurrences, of an exciting order taking shape from organizational chaos.

"When there's too much security, there's too little direct accountability. The reward system does not respond to what people achieve or don't. 'Success' doesn't result directly from what you do.

"Organizations which had become too secure so the basic milieu was one of dull complacency, will do better, will have more creative solutions to their issues, when they are in the mid-range of uncertainty. People produce more and organizations are most creative when there is pressure to perform and people are able to do it."

The Psychological Factor

The language of leadership entails many aspects, chief among which is an understanding of power, of politics, of persuasion, and of psychology. Bardwick is one leader who has come to terms with anxiety; she is familiar enough to see both its positive and its negative facets. She has formulated ways to optimize its impact.

"Organizations can not prosper if there is too much anxiety. But they also need *some*, because without it, there is apathy. There's an optimum point on the anxiety curve. Too little and people are not motivated to perform; too much and they're unable to perform.

"Naturally, many people feel very anxious. They don't know what's going to happen to them and they don't have much control over it either. Uncertainty leads to anxiety. Unremitting anxiety is psychologically extremely costly, so it results in efforts to create security by avoiding risk and resisting change. We see it when people resist innovation, fight to keep their turf, fight to keep things the way they've always been."

Practice: Consider the psychological insights (or lack thereof) evinced in the following memo, in which a general manager is informing her middle managers (three of whom have no training whatsoever in the area of finance or accounting) of the need to undertake departmental budgeting. In the past, the budget process had been handled entirely by the accounting department, with the general manager's input.

As you read, determine if the superior succeeded in allaying fear and optimizing anxiety for her subordinates.

> One new policy that evolved from the annual directors meeting last week was the shift of budgeting from the accounting department to each of the managers. This decentralized approach should give each of you greater control over the allocations of funds for your department's needs. The budgetary projections, complete with amortization-of-equipment costs and allocations for contingencies, are due at the end of March. If you are unfamiliar with the process, check with someone in accounting.

You may wish to analyze comparable memos circulated from the upper echelons of your own organization.

The Synthesis Factor

Bardwick engages in Janusian thinking as she examines the two extremes of anxiety and their related effects upon employees. Excessive security leads to complacency, to the feeling that there will be no negative consequences for the employee, regardless of what he does in the performance of his job, regardless of what critical skills he may or may not possess.

Excessive stress or uncertainty, on the other hand, can lead to paralysis, to a reluctance to initiate because doing so would mean drawing attention to one's self. By juxtaposing these polar opposites, by regarding both the thesis and the antithesis, Bardwick arrives at a synthesis or workable solution, namely, that the mid-range of anxiety produces the vibrancy required for organizational survival.

At a time when job satisfaction and employee commitment are dropping to alarming levels, such vibrancy is required. Employees need to realize that organizational fat has to be expunged in order for the new, lean company to survive. And this very leanness will mean employees will have a chance to acquire and use broader skills, making them even more valuable.

This reshaped firm can produce optimal anxiety and productivity by virtue of its burgeoning existence. But what of the more mature firm, which may have long ago lost its sense of excitement and vitality and which may not be undergoing personnel liposuction?

Says Bardwick, with a wisdom born of backgrounds in both psychology and management counsulting:

"Turning a mature, stable organization back into a vibrant one requires overt acts by top management. Executives must do some fine-tuning. Specifically, they must:

1. Determine where the organization is in terms of panic or apathy.

2. If the mood is primarily apathetic, some level of tension must be constructed. That's done by creating significant positive or negative outcomes as a result of performance. There has to be an institutional response to what people do and that response must have some clout.

3. If the mood is overly anxious, then anxiety must be reduced by lowering uncertainty. Very simply, uncertainty is reduced when people are told what's going on and what will happen to them. In the vacuum of no news, people imagine the worse. Since disappointment is much easier to handle than anxiety, then, good news or bad, honesty is honestly the best policy.

4. If the basic emotional tone of the organization was altered through dramatic change, a period of emotional decompression, of getting back on keel, is necessary. The object of this period is to allow emotion to level off. In this transition state, the survivors, those who made it through the changes, may need a lot of supportive attention.

5. After the emotional level is brought closer to its optimum midpoint, the organization must create a future for itself and for its employees. Institutional goals or an organizational vision must be formulated, articulated, and broadcast with missionary enthusiasm. The goals must be clear, worthwhile, measurable and achievable. This is the beginning of the transition from institutional defensiveness to organizational initiative."

In her delineation of the prescription for resuscitating an aging, ailing organization, Bardwick is sharing her vision. Her leadership language is replete with the clarity she specifies as necessary for restoring vibrancy to the organization.

Practice: Write a five-step prescription for revitalizing your own organization. If yours is a firm or institution which is already at the ideal mid-range of anxiety which Bardwick endorses, write a five-step plan for maintaining that proper balance between panic and apathy.

Pay special attention to the need to find ways of bringing satisfaction to individuals who are used to receiving promotions every few years and who will no longer be able to expect such recognition.

The Optimism Factor

As we have noted earlier, the language of leadership is the language of optimism. Not only does the leader believe her endemic vision can become pandemic but she also believes she can shape the future by instituting that vision in the present.

Bardwick's exhortation to push power down leaves us feeling optimistic about the result of that push:

"Actually, despite all the wrenching changes that have been happening, when I look at the potential for positive gains, I feel optimistic. The pain that is now being generated by early plateauing holds the potential for getting organizations to do what they always should have done, but didn't. Facing the plateauing issue squarely, broadening the definition of success, giving more people the opportunity to be winners, responding to what's actually done by paying for performance and punishing the lack of it...

"Pushing power down and making people responsible and accountable will result in organizations that can compete, can innovate, can flourish. That is the human basis for an economic future."

There are others who also find cause for optimism. Social scientists who have been studying the force of baby-boomerism upon the national character find that this generation is more concerned with job autonomy than job security, with acquiring transportable skills which can take them into many possible positions with many different companies. If such is truly the case, then the job-security problems facing the restructured organization are not as insurmountable as they might have seemed at first.

Practice: About what business-related issues do you feel optimistic? Record your thoughts here. Use language, as Bardwick does, which is clear, honest and optimistic.

In the next chapter, we shall consider the writing of Judy Columbus, who explores power from a different perspective: not the power that corporations can push down to individuals, but rather the power which individuals can bring unto themselves.

CHECKLIST

☐ Do my communications reflect contemporary thought on important issues?

☐ Have I given thought to the emotional or psychological effect of this document or speech upon my audience?

☐ Do I have the requisite data for supporting my point of view?

☐ Can I formulate an easy-to-remember interpretation for those data (like The Rule of 99)?

☐ Do I have a "turnaround" phrase I can use when needed?

☐ Do my messages to co-workers contain a challenge?

☐ Do my words suggest a willingness to take appropriate risks?

☐ Have I given thought to the current buzz words and formed a proper perspective about them?

☐ Do I offer alternatives for the criticism I express?

☐ Is clarity evident in my spoken and written words?

☐ Do I maintain optimism in my interpersonal communications?

Footnotes

22 "Views from the Top," Reprinted with permission, *Business Month* magazine, (July/August, 1988), pp. 66-70. Copyright © 1988 by Goldhirsh Group, Inc., 38 Commercial Wharf, Boston, MA 02110.

23 Kaye, Beverly L., *Up Is Not the Only Way: a Guide for Career Development Practitioners* (New York: Prentice Hall, 1982), p. 241. Reprinted with permission of author.

24 Posner, Mitchell, J., *Executive Essentials* (New York: Avon Books, 1982), pp. 239-240. Copyright © 1982 by Mitchell Posner. Used by arrangement with Avon Books.

CHAPTER SIX:
The Language of Entrepreneurship: A Study of Judy Columbus' Words

> *The secret of success is constancy to purpose.*
> Benjamin Disraeli

Introduction

In this chapter, we shall consider the leadership language of Realtor Judy Columbus, who heads a staff of 19 sales associates and four office management personnel—all women—in Rochester, New York. This highly successful group has sales and listings in excess of $50 million, averaging close to $3 million per sales associate.

When she established her company in 1978, Columbus sought to form a corporation with "dynamic people set in a competitive environment conducting business in a spirit of affection, confidence and trust." Columbus has gone beyond that goal to found the Home Town Funding Company mortgage firm, and to engage in community and charitable activities.

The recipient of numerous leadership awards, Columbus is a frequent lecturer and speaker for various professional organizations. "What It Takes To Be a Leader" is an address delivered to an audience at Nazareth College. In sharing her ideas about management skills with women, Columbus advises them to reach for the top without stepping on others. She advises women not to listen to those who suggest that the vertigo induced by being at the uppermost heights is a solid reason for not climbing the ladder of success.

Define Your Terms

"How many a dispute could have been deflated into a single paragraph if the disputants had dared to define their terms," Aristotle wryly observed 200 years before the birth of Christ. Today's leaders would do well to remember his words, for it is by defining terms that we lay the groundwork for subsequent meaning. With agreed-upon definitions, disputes are less likely to occur and leaders are more likely to have followers who fully understand the principles to which they are committed.

It is reported that J. Edgar Hoover, reviewing a document submitted to him, was dissatisfied with the margins. "Watch the borders!" he wrote in red ink and returned the report. The subordinate interpreted the remark to mean that Hoover wished additional patrols along the Mexican and Canadian borders. Several weeks and thousands of wasted dollars later, the subordinate learned the true meaning of Hoover's remark.

Consider the clarity and concreteness of Columbus' words:

"What I would like to do this morning is first define our terms—what kind of leaders are we talking about? Then I will share with you my personal background, consider three stages of leadership, ask why more women are not leading, propose what leadership is *not*, and suggest how you might approach leadership roles."

Columbus knows that the vagueness of a new thought must be refined into a definition. (A definition is, as Samuel Butler has remarked, "the enclosing of a wilderness of ideas within a wall of words.")

Practice: If you were about to deliver a speech on leadership, what terms would you wish to define? How *would* you define those terms?

Provide a Structure

Researchers have found that the sharing of information—instruction if you will—is facilitated when the leader provides a framework, an outline or preview of the organizational structure on which the information is built.

The good speaker or instructor paves the way for the audience. In a sense, he provides the skeleton first, and then adds informational meat to those organizational bones. The classic guideline for composing—a five-paragraph essay or a five-hour presentation—is to "tell them what you are going to tell them. Then tell them. Finally, go ahead and tell them what you told them."

This introduction-body-conclusion format should be the structure on which all communications, corporate or otherwise, are built. We see that Columbus has done exactly that: she has prepared her audience for what will follow, suggesting not only that she herself is very organized, but also giving her listeners a conceptual model or anchor on which to secure her words.

Use Questions

The realistic verbal expressions to which we alluded in an earlier chapter can often be structured in the form of questions to clarify, to involve the audience, to cause both the sender and the receiver of messages to focus on common meanings. Columbus uses questions to hone the answers and also the experiences she is about to share with her audience. Those questions lead her to present a no-nonsense, common-sense, realistic response to her topic.

"Why do people follow? Why do they follow *me*? What is *my* leadership about?

"I found that my answers were much less complex than those of the consultants. To me, leadership is a behavior and an attitude. It is a common-sense approach to dealing with people, and it is above all, the Golden Rule.

"Again, the distinction I am making is that we are not discussing the person who is *named* 'leader,' but rather one who through attitude and behavior, acts the leadership role and is viewed as such."

Cite the Real World

There are those who believe, as Aristotle did, that language is very difficult to put into words. And yet the very attempt to define what language is, what *leadership* language is—brings insight and awareness. Ideally, through the arduous process of explaining connotations, subtle shifts will occur in the way we use words.

Consider how Columbus reflects realism by citing real-world experiences. It is to these that the listener can relate, since a thread of commonality is being revealed:

> "Columnist Ellen Goodman, commencement speaker at the University of Pennsylvania, noted that she was the only one on the podium with merely a bachelor's degree and said that she assumed her presence was required as 'an emissary from the real world.' That, then, is why I am here. I have, as they say, 'been there.'"

Later in her address, Columbus again uses an anecdote to achieve both realism and motivation; here are words that are clear and pointed and honest.

> "When an officer at the first bank I called asked me, 'Does your husband support your venture?', I responded, 'Does your wife approve of your being a banker?'"

Practice: What are some real-world experiences that you could cite to illustrate some of your convictions? Describe the experience as well as the belief it reflects. What are some real-world experiences that are usually cited by leaders you admire? What convictions are manifest in those experiences?

Establish Your Identity

In *The Ambitious Woman's Guide to a Successful Career,*[25] Margaret Higginson and Thomas Quick speak of the need for women in particular to stand up and be counted. They caution against being seen as an extension of one's boss; they warn about too heavy a dependence on the organization; they suggest women discuss their ambitions and abilities with the right people.

While Columbus' career path led her to entrepreneurism rather than a corporate position, we nonetheless hear echoes of this same advice.

"To me, leadership means being called aggressive and saying 'thank you.'"

"It means not always being liked."

"It means being risk-taking and results-oriented."

"It means a positive mental attitude that minimizes the losses and adds up the gains."

"It means understanding the job responsibility, then going one step further."

"And for sure, it plays havoc with the myth many women hold that the business world will be fair."

Realistic, honest, yet altruistic, Columbus explores the nature of leadership further:

"I think that leadership is damn difficult! And, I think that it may be easier than ever to become a leader because there are becoming fewer takers. In a recent poll, Yankelowich, Skully and White revealed that 80% of the people interviewed admitted they have been deeply affected by the new narcissism and feel that their own needs for sensation, novelty and ego-fulfillment take precedence over the needs of all other people.

"You sure can't feel *that* way and lead for long."

She questions why leaders continue to blaze new paths, encouraging others to follow.

"Maybe because...as it says in the Dean Whitter ad, 'Why not consider a career where the only one who can stop you from succeeding is yourself?'

"Or because I can select a unique group of professionals I am proud to work with and learn from."

She addresses without apology the reasons women may be giving for their failure to don the leadership mantle:

"Why then don't more women put themselves in positions to feel this success? I think that women *opt* not to lead because they fear success and personalize failures. Because they are more used to being victim than survivor.

"Yes, maybe there is a Cinderella Syndrome and no one takes care of leaders except themselves. Maybe because we have been known to count up our losses, and leaders must look to their gains. Because women can't catch on to how to use people and resources in an appropriate networking manner and because women categorize themselves."

Again, by sharing experiences which truly test one's mettle, Columbus is striking a responsive chord. In essence, she is saying, "I tried it and survived. You can do it, too!" She is a living exemplar of Eleanor Roosevelt's words:

I gain strength, courage, and confidence by every experience in which I must stop and look fear in the face. I say to myself, "I've lived through this and can take the next thing that comes along." We must do the things we think we cannot do.

Practice: Columbus encourages her audience/followers to "leave averageness behind" as they move forward to new experiences, new tests of their potential. Make a list of all the ways in which you feel you are "average." Now make another list, a compilation of traits or qualities or actions which show you how you *can* leave averageness behind.

Take Risks

It is virtually impossible to move up the corporate ladder without being willing to take the risks associated with ascending the next step.

Leaving the security of the current rung is necessary if you are to show others what you can do. Merely possessing potential is not a sufficient condition for success in the corporate realm, as merit in and of itself is not always recognized.

You must tap that potential and make it visible by accepting challenges and taking risks. One way to look at risks is to regard them as bets: you are betting that you can succeed in a given situation, betting that you have enough knowledge or skills or charm or luck to come out ahead. Sooner or later, you will lose a bet, but without being willing to make the bet in the first place, you can never advance to the rarefied strata of success.

There is even a heady exhilaration associated with the daring required to take risks—not wild, unplanned risks but carefully calculated risks which, like Columbus', have at least a 50-50 chance of succeeding.

Practice: Reflect on the major risks you have taken since your career began. What risks have you taken in the last year? What risks would you be willing to attempt in the future?

Does your language reflect this attitude of sureness in the outcome of "bets" you make on yourself?

Circumscribe Abstract Words with Concrete Examples

When we abstract, we tend to use fewer words to describe more experiences. For example, how would you respond if asked to talk about your high school days? Think about it for a moment. Most people would generalize those days in a single sentence or two. We might say, "I hated high school. I had no friends and didn't do well in anything except gym." Or, "That was the best time of my life—no cares, no job, no bills, nothing to worry about except who would be your date on Friday night."

But as we were living those days, we built verbal mountains of trivial details. Millions and millions of words were spoken about our high school experience because we were in the middle of *living* it. Many years later, we can abstract all those days of all those years into a few sentences. We have formed a generalized notion or impression of the effect created by time melting those days into a single, crystallized recollection.

Leaders will lose followers if they depend too much on abstracted words or expressions. The abstraction can simply not capture the poignancy or the specific power of the experience as it was lived. Trial lawyers know this and will draw details out of their clients rather than ask them to encapsulate the experience in an abstracted generalization.

In an accident case, for example, the jury would hardly be swayed by a plaintiff who stated that her injuries were painful. But if she spoke of an excruciating pain which left her nauseous and unable to stand, the jury would have a much clearer picture of the pain.

Emotions are especially difficult to put into words, but we *can* provide our followers with convincing realism if we are willing to supply concrete examples. Watch how Columbus does this with the emotion of fear:

"I was frightened because I had no role model and no previous orientation toward risk. I was not used to depending on others, and in addition, was sure it was wrong to borrow money."

In the use of concrete examples and real-life experiences, the leader is establishing his credibility. He presents himself as one who has done more than talk about what he believes. The theory becomes reality as the leader speaks of actions which substantiate his words.

As we learned in Chapter Three, the use of anecdotes goes a long way toward making the leader a more credible presenter of information. And, as Edward R. Murrow insisted, "To be persuasive, we must be believable. To be believable, we must be credible. To be credible, we must be truthful."

Commit to Helping Others

Many of the women who were interviewed for this book spoke of a desire to help other women. While it might be dangerous to carry this assistance too far (one might be perceived, for example, as being sexist or biased by helping only one sex and not the other), many women subscribe to Gloria Vanderbilt's statement: "I've always believed that one woman's success can only help another woman's success."

Columbus alludes to this connectedness to other women in her description of the emotional impact her weighty decision had upon her state-of-mind.

"Then came Black January, when the magnitude of what I had done hit me at once. Now I was sure if I went ahead, I...would risk our financial future, lose my creativity, and finally, let down the whole women's movement! During this period, my hands were like ice, I couldn't sleep, and I could cry on command."

Practice: The only way to change behavior is to begin by consciously determining what the behavior currently is and what it ideally can become with sufficient practice. Begin to develop your consciousness about commitment and about language by writing down specific points in your career when you were encouraged by the words of a leader. What was the actual verbal exchange which made you cognizant of the leader's commitment to you?

Now, engage in some introspection and identify those instances when you made someone else aware of your commitment to him or her through verbal support (followed by the actions which proved the sincerity of your words).

Stereotypes

By our words we shall be classified. And, within the business world, certain syntactical habits or favorite expressions afford clear insights into the professional person's character and style of thinking. For example, the employee whose language is peppered with sports allusion is likely to be an avid sports fan. The individual whose language includes racial or sexist slurs is likely to have specific prejudices. As you read the following descriptions, honestly evaluate your own professional style and see if it may be portraying any of these stereotypic ways of thinking.

Queen Bee

Columbus is the antithesis of the "Queen Bee." While this entomological epithet refers to women, it could just as easily apply to men, as it alludes to the "successful" individual who has achieved at least part of his or her success because of the efforts of others. The Queen Bee is unwilling to share her power, unwilling to allow the worker or drones into her realm of success. Hers is a natural expectation that others exist to feed her appetites and to attend to her needs. In such individuals, there is no concern for others, let alone a commitment to them. The language of the Queen Bee is filled with first-person singular pronouns.

The Ostrich

Unwilling to tackle confrontation, the Ostrich buries his head in the corporate sand and hopes that all unpleasant issues will quietly go away. This type of person is aware of problems but is not brave enough to address them directly. His non-leadership language is pleasant, to be sure, but it lacks the vigor of honesty and assertion. Ostriches are afraid to tell others what they themselves believe; they are also afraid to assume a leadership stance, which may mean telling others what to do.

Sleeping Beauty

Like her fictional equivalent, the real-world Sleeping Beauty awaits rescue and eternal happiness to be bestowed by some vaguely specified future eventuality of a person. Admittedly, there is nothing wrong with wishing for a better tomorrow, but if there is no action to convert the wish to reality, a good portion of the Beauty's life could be wasted.

Sleeping Beauties give the impression that they could perform better, if only.... While they may not overtly blame others, they seem unwilling to exert effort to realize their potential. Theirs is a passive role; deliverance will come, they seem to suggest, from some external source. Their language is devoid of the kind of can-do faith and optimism that we have seen in the language of real leaders.

Marmeladov

The Dostoevskian antecedent for this modern-day sterotype was a man who compulsively confessed. So great was his guilt, so ineffectual the image he had of himself that he continually apologized for offenses which had significance in his mind only. Certainly, one should never lie about mistakes one has made, but there is seldom a sound rationale for announcing one's sins to the world. The language of Marmeladovs is punctuated with "I'm sorry," "Excuse me," and "Would you mind if...." This type of "professional" has trouble asserting her opinion or asking for her due.

Star/Starlet

This sort of employee enjoys having the spotlight focused on him and will stop short of nothing to obtain that brightness in which he basks. His phototropism needs may even include sexual allusions which will ensure he is noticed. Perhaps insecure about his competence, the star feels he can always attract the attention of people who matter by emphasizing his obvious attractiveness.

These ploys may work in the short run, but no firm can tolerate for very long the performer who relies not on skill but on sexuality.

Puritan

There are those who are task-oriented and those who are people-oriented. Ideally, one is able to alter one's orientation according to the demands of a given situation. The Puritan does not have this flexibility. She possesses such a strong work ethic that she is unable to relax and relate to others on a social level. Social amenities are the glue that holds together the fabric of an organization, but the Puritan lacks the skills for applying this glue. As a result, her conversations and working relationships may seem disjointed.

The Puritan's language is filled with continual references to the task or project on which she is working. Any conversation or action which is not directly related to the accomplishment of a goal is regarded as a waste of time by such individuals. The Puritan's values may work well in crisis-management situations, but at other times, she makes co-workers feel guilty and uncomfortable.

Quidnunc

Quidnunc literally means "What now?" And we find this type of employee spending much valuable time uncovering and replanting the latest news of what is happening in the company. The quidnunc is a one-man or one-woman grapevine, who often stirs up trouble unnecessarily by spreading rumors that are either malicious, unnecessary, or untrue.

You can identify such a stereotype for his language is replete with expressions such as "Did you know...?" "Have you heard...." and "Wait 'til I tell you about...." Harmless gossip is bound to occur in any group of people working together, but the quidnunc exceeds the bounds of propriety and good taste. He is costing the company, in more ways than merely the financial.

Recognize You Are Not Alone in the Pressures You Face

Columbus' language is clearly free from these stereotypic expressions. And while she has nothing in common with Queen Bees or other identifiable types, she does have something in common with women who have succeeded in the business world.

In their study of managerial women who have managed to break through the glass ceiling, Morrison *et al.,* examine how female executives differ from their male counterparts in terms of the types of pressure with which they have had to cope:

> Throughout their careers, they had to operate with three levels of pressure constantly pushing on them. These pressures—of the job itself, of their pioneer role in the job, and of the strain of their family obligations—made their advancement that much harder and that much more remarkable.[26]

Share Personal Revelations

The language Columbus chooses to discuss her leadership role discloses an individual in control of her life, eager to tell others how to acquire a control of their own. Intensely personal in her revelations, Columbus seems to understand how persuasive the sharing of basic human emotions can be.

> "I felt that if I didn't make this move, accept this opportunity, then my past would rule my future, yesterday would become tomorrow. If I did not take this risk, I would limit myself to being what I was; to more or less giving up the process of becoming. I realized this was no longer the time to get opinions from friends and family, but to take control of my life and responsibility for my actions. I was alone and it felt good."

Engage in Self-Appraisal

With her take-charge-of-your-own-life attitude, Columbus parallels Dennis Waitley who views life as a self-fulfilling prophecy: "You won't necessarily get what you want in life, but in the long run you will usually get what you expect."

Practice: Engage in honest self-appraisal right now. Write out what exactly it is that you expect from life. Appraise your strengths as well as your weaknesses and outline the steps you intend to take to help ensure that you will get what you expect. Distinguish, if you can, between what you want from life and what you actually expect.

Opt for Leadership

Columbus repeatedly emphasizes that leaders consciously strive for authority. They *choose* to become who and what they are. But that choice, she tells us, can only come after we have taken stock of ourselves.

"This is what I term Stage 1 of the leadership role and we *all* come to this point at some time. It may occur in your personal life as you decide to take on new responsibilities; in your communal activities as you consider an elected office; or in the workplace as a job opening arises which seems a possibility for you.

"It is that place where you realize that leadership is a choice! That time when you take for granted that there will be risk, there will be aloneness, there will be unfinished work and stressful decision-making. That point where you ask yourself, 'Who am I?' and 'Who do I want to become?' 'Is this move important enough to me?' And, 'How ambitious am I?'

"If you get the right answers, go for it!"

Sherwood's Breakpoints

These pivotal points which take the average person and spin him around in the direction of leadership are similar to the career breakpoints which Andrew Sherwood discusses in his book of the same title.[27]

1. The chance to be relocated
2. A change of command
3. A change in performance appraisal
4. A time when the needs of your company change
5. A change in your productivity or skills
6. An opportunity with attendant risk
7. The completion of a vague cycle in your company
8. A change in your visibility
9. An accumulation of work experience that gives you leverage
10. A salary peak

Tackle Tough Questions

The leader is always on guard for opportunities, is continually deliberating the pro's and con's of situations—breakpoints or otherwise—to learn how circumstances might be used to accomplish organizational aims. Crucial to that deliberation process is the asking of questions—tough questions that others may not dare to ask.

Leadership language does not dance around the issues: it confronts them directly. Even though her audience was comprised of women, Columbus speaks of things women might not wish to hear. She does not hesitate to criticize, as a caring parent would, in the belief that criticism is a prelude to change and action.

> "Facing opportunities to move up, to achieve financial independence, to improve a self-image—with all of this to look forward to, women opt out! They opt out of visibility, risk,

responsibility. They default...setting the stage for one of the other sexes to assume leadership positions. Then they blame the system and look to external causes for their failure."

Practice: What are some aspects of your life or your job with which you are dissatisfied? Can you write honestly about those issues, criticizing, if need be, those forces (perhaps within yourself) which are responsible for the current difficulties?

Use Quotations

Listen to the words of those men and women who have the reputation of being able to affect—through their choice and delivery of words—large numbers of people. You will usually find that the most powerful speakers and writers quote other outstanding individuals. So often, the pithy saying or the appropriate quotation encapsulates an idea or concept, thereby crystallizing the thought in the minds of listeners or readers.

Columbus employs the words of Dr. Alice Sargent—

"We women are basically foreigners in the job world we've entered, an environment where power and profit skills reap the highest rewards."

—to illustrate her point that some skills, the skills with the highest reward, are usually obtained through independent action.

In the course of her speech, she cites the language of other leaders:

Colby Chandler, Chairman of Board and CEO of Eastman Kodak Company:
"Managing change is what a successful business is all about."

Benjamin Hoff, author of **The Tao of Pooh:**
"Isn't the knowledge that comes from experience more valuable than the knowledge that doesn't? It seems fairly obvious

that a lot of scholars need to go outside and sniff around, walk through the grass and talk to the animals."

Richard Marcus, president of Neiman-Marcus Stores:
"If you follow in someone else's footsteps, you never get ahead."

Judith Bardwick, author of **The Psychology of Women:**
"We tend to idealize role models when we are scared or uncertain. Alas, we can be models of what we are, and no more than that."

Continuing to employ quotations to lend depth and substance to her own words, Columbus exhorts her audience to form a leadership philosophy of their own. It should be an uplifting, idealized statement that bespeaks hope, as does this remark by Peter Drucker.

"The purpose of an organization is to have ordinary people do extraordinary things."

Practice: Experts agree that reading outside one's field contributes to the successful person's general knowledge of the world and to her ability to communicate with confidence. In fact, they estimate that 30–40 percent of the reading you do should be in areas beyond the scope of your current job or area of interest/expertise.

From the reading you do, begin to collect quotations which reflect some of your most deeply held convictions about your chosen career field. The individuals you cite may or may not be in that specific field.

Take Action

Although she cites Sargent's views on power and profit skills, Columbus expresses concern about the compilation of skills thought to be necessary in order for leadership to be exercised. Her concern is that some women may regard such a list as a *sine qua non* for leadership. By being too harsh in their judgment of their abilities, women may do irreparable damage to their careers: they may deny themselves the chance to try...simply because they do not possess *all* the skills thought to be requisite for leadership.

"As women," Columbus assures her audience, "we cannot afford all of that caution."

"We can *prepare* for leadership, as John F. Kennedy did before the 1960 election when he listened to the recordings of Winston Churchill's speeches, picking up the grand rhythms of the language. Yes, we can practice leadership principles, but the only way to learn to use them is to lead.

"Not knowing it all is no excuse not to start."

It is all too easy to find the obstacles which might prevent us from reaching our goals. It is more comfortable to remain as we are—sacrificing no security, resisting any change—than to pledge to overcome those obstacles. The leaders are those who bring life to their philosophy by ignoring, circumventing, or plowing right through the barriers that impede others.

Columbus cites the obstacles which might have thwarted her entrepreneurial aspirations: not having a mentor, not having a role model, not having the experience. She then rejects these excuses which women sometimes employ as "outs," ready reasons why they dare not try.

"I stand before you to state openly that a mentor, role model or supportive husband is not a requisite in order for leadership to take place. We do not need permission to begin."

Declare Entitlement

Columbus empowers herself. She unequivocally declares that she is entitled to her share of the success pie, the primary ingredient of which is the ability to take charge, if not of others, at least of one's self. And, she invites other to do the same. The overall effect of this assuredness resembles the tone of Whitman's "Song of Myself":

"I celebrate myself, and sing myself,
And what I assume you shall assume,
For every atom belonging to me as good
    belongs to you."

Leaders recognize worth; they know that worth must be employed if America is to use her most important resources. These values must be communicated, Columbus maintains. The first recipient of the knowledge may well be one's self:

"We must know what we want for ourselves, must be able to state it, and if necessary, ask for the support we need. Our first sales pitch may be to ourselves. Once we have identified the goal, we have begun."

Before we can communicate leadership principles to others, we must first communicate with ourselves.

Find New Challenges

Renewal is important to leaders. And that renewal so often comes from exposure to the words and ideas of others. The leader synthesizes disparate ideas to which he has been exposed and fashions for himself and others a carefully articulated vision of new directions in which to travel.

Mindful of this rejuvenating ability, Columbus cites the self-deprecating comment of Yves St. Laurent, "Before each opening, I am nothing" in an attempt to remind us that a leader needs to create himself anew, to find new opportunities, to rest—not on past laurels—but on future laudations (which will then become past laurels themselves).

Leaders tend to view competition as a stimulus for action, rather than as a devastating condition which paralyzes spirits and behaviors. High-performers are competitive, candid, and in possession of high self-esteem.

Practice: It is hoped that this book has caused you to re-examine some of your own behaviors and views. By now you may even be ready to bring about some changes in your life—at least as far as your career is concerned. We all have to plan for change and that planning inevitably involves a consideration of the future.

Make a list of the various ways in which you can **take action** in order to move your goals from the dreamable to the do-able stage. Think, too, about those benefits or conditions to which you have every right to aspire; **declare entitlement** and do not permit organization-imposed or self-imposed barriers to impede your course. If you have not made significant progress in your profession within the last three years, it may be time for you to **find new challenges**. Think deeply about what those challenges or opportunities might be and prepare a list to which you can refer on a regular basis.

Develop a Philosophy

Why is it important to articulate what you believe about what you are doing? Apart from Plato's insistence that the life which is unexamined is not worth living, the very process of attempting to mold your ideas, to fashion a statement which represents your idealized aims or hopes for what your organization can accomplish—this process enables us to ascertain what we truly think. Having this belief or philosophy in front of you will help, in obvious and also in subtle ways, as you move toward your defined ambitions.

You may be asked in interviews what your business philosophy is. Have one ready, not only for such occasions but also as a touchstone for aligning career moves with self-designed criteria.

You might ask a company executive what he or she believes the firm's business philosophy is and then determine how closely that response parallels your own.

If your job requires you to supervise a number of subordinates, it is especially important for you to be able to share a philosophy with those whose professional efforts you oversee.

Columbus, in encouraging women to reach for the top, very simply states,

"You need to form a philosophy because that is what commands the commitment from those who follow, those who will make you a leader. You must be able to articulate to them what you are trying to achieve and their part in the plan.

"Will you have a value-based policy? Will there be moral considerations to your decisions? Will you do unto others *as* they do unto you—or *before* they do unto you? Is their growth as important as your own?

"This is the time when you need to dream a little. How do you envision yourself in this new role? What do you need to do to make the transition comfortable?

Practice: These questions will aid you in refining your philosophy:

1. Write brief descriptions of three situations in your life when you performed at your best.

2. Having done that, identify which factors or conditions may have been common to all three situations.

3. What is your ideal work style?

4. What would you describe as a job opportunity?

5. What causes you to feel job satisfaction? Job stress?

6. What are your priorities in life?

7. To what single factor do you attribute your current success? What other factors do you think are necessary to get ahead?

Assess Your Capabilities

Putting leadership into practice from this very moment forward requires you to ask yourself such questions, to do a thorough self-assessment. If you have already engaged in this frank appraisal of your abilities on an earlier occasion, it may be time to reassess, to decide if new skills have been acquired, and if noted deficiencies have been overcome or compensated for.

As Columbus urges,

"After defining a philosophy of your own leadership, you need to take a personal inventory, noting strengths and weaknesses which you bring to the job. A weakness is not 'no role model.' A weakness is 'no past experience with financial analysis.' And the solution is to hire an expert or to study accounting. The attitude underlying this survey is 'What do I do well? How can I maximize my potential? Where do I need shoring up, and how can I best accomplish this?' Fears fall into perspective as we value our leadership strengths."

From this analysis should come a clearer sense of purpose, a road map of the direction in which you should be moving and the pitfalls of which you should be aware. The leader is one who is fully cognizant of the possibilities (both prospects and pitfalls) that lie before him.

Establish Lifetime Goals

Consider, for example, the possibilities which an adventurer named John Goddard has made into realities. When he was 15, Goddard established 127 challenging lifetime goals for himself. To date, he has accomplished 107 of those desires and has traveled over one million miles in the process. In the course of reifying his dreams, Goddard has experienced unique achievements such as exploring the world's longest river or setting flight records.

Turning dreams into reality is the end-product of philosophy-determining and capabilities-assessing. In meeting established goals, the leader must be willing to rise above hurdles set by others or by circumstances. The leader is steadfast in ignoring boundaries or pragmatic questions or traditional confines. She forgets about what her skills will permit her to do; she puts aside questions of what the organization will allow her to do. She vows to break free of self-limiting restraint words such as "never" or "can't" or expressions such as "We always do it this way."

Reach Higher than You Think You Can

When undertaking these, and similar goal-setting exercises, remind yourself that performance researchers believe that the average person can accomplish 40 or 50 percent more than he thinks he can. Our brains have the capacity to learn and use 40 different languages or to memorize a set of encyclopedias. Yet few of us ever vow to take full advantage of that power.

Prepare a Catastrophe Report

Charles Garfield, who has studied peak performers for over 20 years, encourages people to fill out a Catastrophe Report—a consideration of all the things that might go wrong with a given plan. Being able to actually articulate the worst-possible scenario that would ensue from taking a risk helps most individuals to realize that their highest ambitions *can* be achieved and the consequences of a mistake or poor decision would not be disastrous in most cases.

When thinking about the risks or challenges that you might tackle, think first about the positive consequences of pursuing that risk. Then itemize the negative consequences. If you do not feel you could live with the worst possible eventuality, you should abandon that particular risk in its current form.

Remain Centered

Columbus points out that leaders must be flexible; they must be willing to employ the style that best meets each situation and the individuals in it. Her description of the idealized self is a fine example of the juxtaposition of Janusian terms:

"You see that there are times to be intense, and others to be casual; the need to be part pragmatist-part dreamer; self-assured yet with an openness to learn from experience; ego-centered with a desire to advance others; spontaneous, yet organized; highly independent, yet the best team player. You must communicate clearly and listen well; succeed humbly and handle failure."

Studies of derailed executives have found that an inability to adapt to change was one of the reasons fast-trackers, seemingly destined for success, never reached the top of the career ladder. Everything changes and the leader must be able to move with the times. Strategies that may have worked in the past may not work so well today. Skills that served a purpose in the beginning of your career may have little relevance for your current position. Work patterns that helped you function efficiently at one point may need redefinition at this point.

Seize the Moment

The leader, while striving for perfectionism, must occasionally forego it in order to put a plan into action. Perfectionism can lead to postponement and ultimately to paralysis. In her attempt to ensure that no stone has been left unturned, that every contingency has been anticipated and provided for, the leader may actually sacrifice the most opportune moment for action.

In speaking of the early period during which leadership techniques are being tested and selected, Columbus advises:

"You may learn during this period that plans not yet perfected need to be put into practice. Mistakes can be corrected and refinements made later. Realize that few decisions are set into concrete and that the ability to think clearly is essential to commanding the respect of others. Get a track record for risk-taking. This will, like magic, open up new areas of living to you and will set an example for those following."

Practice: Pay close attention to the decision-making style of those around you. Compare it to your own. How do the most effective people make their determinations? How long do they usually take? Do they depend on the advice of others? How do they handle the need to decide, when all the information is not available? When decisions are poor, how serious are the after-effects? What do these individuals do to counter the effects of unwise decisions?

Consult with Others

No one has it all, no one knows it all, Columbus asserts. And, for those areas in which you have little proficiency, you need merely turn to those who do. Even the President, after all, has an extensive staff of advisors.

"When you need them, hire specialists, the best professionals available. Women are used to the phrase, 'I can do it myself' and they carry this motto into the job world. But 'Super-woman' is either dead or dying!"

Listen to the leadership language displayed by Columbus as she continues sharing success strategies. Each sentence is an imperative sentence, beginning with a strong action verb.

"Get yourselves the backup you need in personal or career lives to do the job you need to do. Talk to other leaders—the best are the most willing to share ideas. Select the traits of those you admire and add them to your style, as Maxwell Maltz advises: 'Imagine how you would feel if you were successful. Then feel that way right now.'"

Practice: You have itemized your strengths and weaknesses in an earlier practice exercise. Return to that list and beside each weakness or deficiency, try to record some way to overcome the deficit. If you can, write down the name of someone to whom you might turn (or hire) for information or assistance.

Maintain Your Motivation

There are certain personality traits that will probably not lead to successful undertakings. Such qualities as being dependent or passive or docile are not associated with leaders. Nor are submissiveness, a lack of self-confidence, or a lack of direction.

These traits are the opposite of what we hear and see in the words of Judy Columbus. Here is a woman who is able to go beyond the negative, to reach deep within herself to that inner core of strength which enables her—and other entrepreneurs—to keep on going, despite setbacks and fears and adversity. She tells us:

"A leader needs to be 'up.' A positive attitude is synonymous with leadership. She needs to be nourished to maintain this perspective and that is where the importance of associations comes in. A leader should be with those who motivate her, and in places where inspiration exists."

Leaders do not depend, at least not exclusively, on inspiration from external sources:

"When you spend the day at a motivation workshop with a hot-shot sent in from Phoenix with attache case, jokes and uplifting statements, this is a tremendous upper—for about 24 hours. What is more important is the ability to refresh and elevate yourself and your thinking on a daily basis. You will find that your spirit can be contagious."

Make Your Leadership Skills Lifeskills

Why seek to develop leadership? Apart from the advantages that accrue to one's career from the demonstrated ability to persuade others to work toward intended results, what does the practice of continuous small acts of leadership do for the development of one's character and the accomplishment of organizational aims?

There is an undeniable satisfaction that comes from the application of leadership. The leader feels a kind of power, it is true, in knowing that his words were able to lead others to work in unison to complete a mission, a mission that the leader has described as being important enough to call forth this concerted effort.

This power is a mature power, not the kind of puerile power associated with those who try to exert dominance over every person they come in contact with—from subordinates to waiters in a restaurant. The latter kind of power is a game, a need to assert one's ego and one's will upon unsuspecting victims for the mere pleasure of being victorious in insignificant ways. Certainly, you can develop your power-skills in other, more meaningful ways.

There is no denying that leadership is closely affiliated with power. The power muscles are flexed, however, not in the interest of self-aggrandizement, but rather in the interest of reaching goals that matter to a number of people.

Leadership language means honestly leading others to implement changes designed to ultimately better the organization. There will be a carry-over of the skills the leader uses in the workplace to other areas of his life.

As Columbus advises:

"Leadership skills are lifeskills, and those that serve you well in the office are equally important in the rest of your life."

Clearly, the traits we have identified and the skills you are being urged to acquire will transfer over to the way you conduct your life in general. These professional praxes, in time, will serve as guideposts for leadership behavior.

Practice: Reflect on the events of the last several weeks and try to isolate a situation from your personal life in which you manifested some of the leadership skills you admire in others. In the months ahead, make note of those occasions when you do manage to meld the business-world skills and the personal-realm need for such skills. Acknowledge your growing competence each time.

In the next chapter, we shall analyze how Gannett Newspapers editor Barbara Henry demonstrates leadership language as she addresses somewhat controversial issues with her audience.

CHECKLIST

☐ Have I defined those terms that are integral to the thrust of my communication?

☐ Is my document or speech well-organized, beginning with an overview of the structure?

☐ Have I used questions in appropriate places?

☐ Have I used real-world examples to make the information more relevant?

☐ Have I used concrete illustrations to explain abstract terms?

☐ Does the document or speech reflect a willingness to help others?

☐ Are my communications devoid of the stereotypes described in this chapter?

☐ Are there some personal revelations with which the audience can identify?

☐ Have I addressed or avoided difficult issues?

☐ Have I benefited from the wisdom of others by using quotations in the text of my message?

☐ Does my message contain a recommendation for action?

☐ Do my communications reflect a willingness to take appropriate risks?

☐ Do I offer challenges to others as a way of energizing them?

Footnotes

[25] Higginson, Margaret and Thomas Quick. *The Ambitious Woman's Guide to a Successful Career* (Ann Arbor: Book Demand, UMI Publishers, 1980).

[26] *Breaking the Glass Ceiling,* © 1987 by Ann M. Morrison, Randall P. White, Ellen Van Velsor. From page 15. Reprinted with permission of Addison-Wesley Publishing Company, Inc., Reading, Massachusetts.

[27] Sherwood, Andrew. *Breakpoints* (New York: Doubleday), 1986. Reprinted with permission.

CHAPTER SEVEN:
The Language of Journalism: A Study of Barbara Henry's Words

> *"You are always in command of a situation where you control the communication system."*
> Betty Lehan Harragan

Introduction

Barbara Henry's path to editorship represents a straight and narrow journey...one she has been on for 16 years. Even though she has passed significant mileposts along the way, she still looks forward to tackling new challenges, addressing other issues, adapting to the future's advent.

Her speech to a women's group ends with remarks that reveal this spirit of adventure, this acceptance of change:

"Newspapers have changed in how we report, in how we edit, in how we look. It's likely that we'll change a lot more in the 30 years I have left in this business.

"Some futurists predict that by the time I retire in 2017, there won't be newspapers any more. We'll receive all our news electronically.

"I certainly hope they're wrong—and not only for selfish reasons of job security, although that's certainly one of them. I want newspapers to be around so I can come back to the Chatterbox Club 30 years from now and give a speech with the same title as tonight's—how newspapers have changed."

A journalism major at the University of Nevada-Reno, Henry's first job was with a Reno newspaper (which was subsequently purchased by Gannett). She moved up the ranks to editor in the city where Gannett newspapers were born: Rochester, New York.

Warm Up the Audience

Henry begins her address, as did Iacocca, Cuomo and Peters, with remarks designed to establish rapport from the outset. She displays humility, self-revelation and a "concede" approach with comments such as these.

> "I was a little intimidated because I knew Gene Dorsey would be here. And he's a master public speaker.

> "When I finally got over the fact that you would be able to compare my performance with Gene's, Rita called again to tell me Vince Spezzano would be here, too. Besides being my boss, Vince is also known for his public speaking ability.

> "Unfortunately, I'm not known for my speaking ability like Gene and Vince. They're the lucky exceptions to the general rule about newspaper journalists who, like me, tend to be more comfortable behind a typewriter than in front of an audience."

Use Transitions

Henry compliments her audience, an "impressive group," and then voices her opinion about what journalists should do. By pointing a critical finger at her own profession, she increases the likelihood that her audience will later be more willing to accept remarks she makes in defense of her profession. (Her audience, in this case, is also her readership.)

> "...Even though newspaper editors might not be comfortable in front of an audience, we should be doing a lot more of it. Instead of sitting in the comfortable insulation of a newsroom, where I only have to be face to face with fellow journalists. These opportunities give me a chance to be face to face with our readers."

She uses the word "readers" as a natural transition to the thrust of her presentation:

"Many of our readers wonder why we do the things we do—or why we don't do things they think we should do. Sometimes, we don't give them enough of a chance to ask."

Practice: Try writing a speech-beginning by following the same sequence Henry does: self-critical comment, introduction of transition words, and use of transition words to introduce real topic.

Have a Strong Opinion

In discussing the language of leadership, Henry pointed to research concerning a listening audience: 7 percent of the total message is comprised of the words themselves; 55 percent of the message by what the speaker looks like; and 38 percent of the total message received depends on what the speaker sounds like. She advises speech-givers to "have a presence," which includes speaking in a firm, clear voice.

"Presence" also means, declares Henry, having strong opinions. In this excerpt from her remarks to the Chatterbox Club, she takes a strong stand on journalists' rightful areas of inquiry. She feels fully justified in having this opinion, and so uses a "compel" approach.

"Let's start with covering the personal lives of candidates. I don't know about you, but when I make a decision to vote for a candidate, the first considerations I have are: Is he or she honest? Is he or she decent? Does he or she have common sense? Do I feel comfortable with this person?

"I guess the most personal the press has gotten in recent memory is our coverage of Gary Hart. If you're running for President, is it anyone's business whether you're cheating on your wife?

"Is it a story if it's common knowledge among reporters in Washington and Colorado that Gary Hart has been cheating on his wife for years? Should reporters who are covering an election keep that to themselves—as they did in the past?

"Some would say, no, it's not a story. Reporters should keep it to themselves. In fact, I got calls from people telling me just that. I had to disagree.

"If a Presidential candidate is a known womanizer and he lies about it, I think it's a story. It tells me something about those qualities I look for in a candidate: honesty, decency and common sense. It wasn't too long ago that newspapers would never think of reporting that a Presidential candidate was cheating on his wife. Now, it's news.

"However, I do think it's going too far to ask a candidate randomly if he or she has ever committed adultery, which seemed to be happening during the Hart flap."

Leadership language is predicated on strong opinions. Listen to the assertion made by Peter Drucker in his opening comments about the key to success. His audience here is the *Wall Street Journal* readership.[28] (The column in its entirety can be found at the end of this chapter.)

"Some businesses—not very many—get a fiftyfold, or even a hundredfold, return on the research dollar. Many more get little or nothing. The key to success is not knowledge, intelligence or hard work—and least of all, luck. It is following the 10 Rules of Effective Research.

1. Every new product, process or service begins to become obsolete on the day it first breaks even.

2. Thus, your being the one who makes your product, process or service obsolete is the only way to prevent your competitor from doing so."

Admit Mistakes

As she was unafraid to tackle thorny issues, Henry is also unafraid to admit the Fourth Estate sometimes goes too far.

"Now, lest you think I'm up here to defend everything we do as perfect, let's talk about Dan Quayle's military record and the question about our coverage being negative.

"The initial question to Dan Quayle about his National Guard service during the war was valid. It's an obvious question—especially to Vietnam veterans who did go to Southeast Asia.

"But I think once he answered it, reporters dragged it out. Every appearance he made it came up. I got sick of it and I think readers and viewers did, too. Once everyone has the information and his response, they can decide for themselves if it will be a factor in the way they vote.

"Basically, it was probably a case of some lazy reporting. It was easier to get yet another story on his National Guard service than to research his record after 12 years in Congress."

Practice: Defend a position you have held or an action you have taken. Do not be afraid to admit you have made a mistake, but make certain, throughout your piece, that you are letting your strong opinions be heard.

Avoid Sexist Language

Both men and women are guilty of using it, Henry points out. She finds her reporters, regardless of sex, will sometimes refer to women with physical-appearance descriptors, while they refer to men with attributes of power. For example, a woman may be described as "petite" or "well-groomed," while a man might be described as "an imposing figure." Henry encourages her staff—photographers as well as reporters—to be equitable in their pictorial and verbal references.

Avoid Soft Language

There are words that are considered "soft" and words that are considered "hard." Regardless of your sex, you should avoid the soft words. Quite simply, they do not demonstrate leadership language. The difference is quite apparent in the following list.

SOFT	HARD
lovely	outstanding
Scootch over a teeny bit.	Move over.
darling, adorable, gorgeous	attractive
Forgive me. I didn't mean that.	You misunderstood.
Would you be so kind as to hand me that pen?	Please hand me that pen.

It is especially apparent in a phrase such as "I'm so sorry that you didn't receive the merit increase." The speaker is assuming some guilt or responsibility for something totally outside his control. It would have been much better to have said, "It's too bad you didn't receive the merit increase this time." The second expression reflects an external locus of control; it is also less damning, for it suggests that the person will probably receive one in the future.

Soft language embeds adjectives and adverbs in its structure; **hard language has more nouns and verbs peppering its syntax.** Consider this anecdote from Henry's speech; it is laden with nouns and verbs.

"I have a friend who's the editor of the *Louisville Courier-Journal*. His father was a laborer and he grew up on the less affluent side of town.

"He likes to tell the story of how one day, it was snowing in Louisville. Snow in Louisville is rare, so it is a big story. The editor got up from his chair, walked out into the newsroom, cupped his hands over his mouth and yelled for all to hear, 'It's snowing on the west side of the city.'

"Then he walked back into his office and sat down. His message was clear. He wanted his reporters and photographers—most of whom lived on the other side of town—to go to a place they don't normally go to get pictures and quotes about the weather.

"We're trying to do the same thing. We want our coverage to reflect the entire community—not just the neighborhoods and interests of the majority of our editors and writers."

Soft language is more emotional, more polite, more complimentary, and more indirect. **Hard language is honest and forceful and bold.** This selection from Drucker's column for the *Wall Street Journal* has that leadership-language hardness:

"Research is separate work, but it is not a separate function. Development—the translation of research results into products, processes and services that can be manufactured, sold, delivered and serviced—must go hand in hand with research. And manufacturing, marketing and service all affect research from the beginning, just as much as the results of research in turn affect them. In the university, research may be the search for new knowledge as an end in itself. In industry, in government, and in medicine, research is the search for new utility."

Soft language equivocates, hesitates, it beats around the bush. **Hard language is matter-of-fact.** As Henry said during her interview, "If I have an opinion, I express it. I can be blunt if I need to be." Hers is not a waffling style.

"We are working to increase the number of Blacks and Hispanics who cover the news and edit it. Currently, about 11 percent of our news staff are members of minority groups and about 40 percent are women. More diversity on the staff means more diversity in our news columns. And that's a major change in newspapers in general, not just ours. It's definitely a change for the better."

Soft language uses an inductive approach; **hard language is deductive—it moves from the top down.** The leader knows that people are busy and that they will appreciate efficiency in language. And so, she employs a bottom-line-first approach, filling in the details after the point has been made. You have, no doubt, listened to a non-leader (or read something such a person wrote) and wondered, "What is the point?" Using hard language means getting right to the point.

Drucker uses hard language in the following dictum:

"Effective research requires organized abandonment—not only of products, processes and services, but also of research projects. Every product, process, service and research project needs to be put on trial for its life every few years, with this question: 'Would we now start this product, process, service, or research project, knowing what we know now?"

Soft language encourages self-indulgence; **hard language encourages self-starting**. Henry includes in her address an excerpt from a newspaper article about the members of the Chatterbox Club (written 60 years ago) in which they are depicted as pampered society women. Henry's audience no doubt appreciated her refutation of that image:

"That was 60 years ago. If we published that today, the pickets would be out in front of Exchange Boulevard and I would deservedly be run out of town on a rail by a group of angry women. You all probably would be among them. Chatterbox Club members didn't lie abed until the middle of the morning then and they don't now."

Soft language puts qualifiers at the end of statements. **Hard language makes its point without obsequiousness or apology.** The verbal tags that are placed at the end of a sentence diminish the strength of the sentence's assertion. They qualify or dilute the thrust of the thought.

For example, "Let's get this under way by Friday" suggests a forward movement. It sounds as if someone has taken charge and is rallying others around a common purpose.

Now look at the same sentence with a simple tag at the end: "Let's get this under way by Friday, okay?" The word "okay" suggests that the leader is seeking permission from the others rather than issuing an exhortive command.

Practice: Begin making a list of all the tags you hear in the speech of colleagues. Do this for one full week. Then

conscientiously seek to avoid using such phrases yourself, as they will rob your language of power. Here are a
few of the most common tags: Okay. Isn't it? Doesn't
he? Won't she?

Children often put qualifiers at the beginning of their sentences, as
if they need to secure your attention before proceeding. Phrases such
as "You know what?" or "Guess what!" or "You know what happened
to me today?" are used to secure the adult's interest and commitment
to continuing the conversation. Such verbal ploys, however, are not
found in the language of leaders, for they bespeak a dependency on
the approval of others. These qualifiers make the speaker sound vulnerable or powerless.

Similarly, soft language says "no" in such a way that it sounds like
"maybe" or even "yes." **Hard language is definite; it says "no" as a
means of exercising the right to make a judgment on a request. It
does not apologize.**

Henry was recently faced with the need to say "no" to a member of
her reading public:

"I got a call from a retired Kodak employee recently. He said,
'Frank Gannett would turn over in his grave if he knew what
you were reporting about Kodak. [The Eastman Kodak company was founded in Rochester. It was recently accused of con-
taminating the groundwater near one of its facilities.]
Rochester depends on Kodak. You're hurting the company that
this community relies on for its existence.'"

Knowing she might have touched a sensitive nerve in the body
of her audience, Henry quickly took an offensive stance in order to
supply a sound defense or rationale for her reporting actions.

"Perhaps some of you are thinking the same thing. To be
honest with you, I get upset when someone accuses the
newspapers of trying to tear down the institutions of this community. ...It just isn't true.

"The Kodak chemical contamination story is a tough one. Kodak has 45,000 employees here. Rochester does depend on Kodak, as my caller correctly pointed out.

"Kodak is a big supporter of better education. Kodak is a big contributor to the cultural amenities that make Rochester so special. That's why, when our reporter discovered the problem of contamination of the groundwater around Kodak Park last March, we took very seriously the responsibility we have to report it. We knew the effect it would have."

In the interview, Henry expanded: "It would have been irresponsible of us *not* to have reported the possible contamination of drinking water."

Henry prides herself on having presented a balanced view of the situation:

"Both Vince and I have taken a special and personal interest in what's reported on our news pages and what's said on our editorial pages on this subject.

"Vince and I have met with Kodak executives twice to discuss the coverage. If you look at our coverage as a whole over the past six months—and I have many times—it has been balanced and fair. In fact, we praised Kodak on our editorial page for its quick and generous offers to homeowners."

Practice: Think about a situation in which you took (or perhaps should take) an unpopular stand, one that may run contrary to prevalent thinking. Prepare a persuasive argument (in this case, using an inductive approach) to convince an audience that yours was a responsible approach. Be balanced in your account, but do not fail to lead your audience, point by point, to the conviction you hold on the issue.

Soft language is inert language, not at all like the language we see quoted above. **Hard language is rousing language; it is action-oriented.**

Henry used the 60-year-old story about the Chatterbox Club as a segue to the changes newspapers have undergone. She then uses the same theme of change to segue into coverage of political stories. Listen to the energy in the following:

"But newspapers were different then. First, in 1929, there were no women in newsrooms to prevent this kind of stereotyping from getting into print. Now, there are plenty of women working in and running newsrooms.

"Second, sensitivities have changed. You just can't take that type of license in a news story.

"Many other things have changed in this business, too—not just the way we depict women."

Soft language is passive, lifeless. **Hard language is colorful, concrete.** The leader thinks about which words will have impact on her audience. For example, "Our coffee comes from Columbia" does not have quite the same allure as "Our mountain-fresh coffee is grown on the hills of Columbia."

Practice: Assume you have to deliver presentations to the following types of audiences. What images or metaphors would you use to appeal to their basic traits?

Example: An audience that values freedom would respond to images of a bird soaring in the skies.

An audience that is conservative.

An audience that is young and fun-loving.

An audience that is composed of senior citizens.

An audience that is composed of educators.

An audience that is business-oriented.

Soft language is insipid, vague; it does not take a stand. **Hard language is incisive and specific.** Note how Henry does not equivocate in her speech. Here is what she had to say about her career.

"I've always told people I worked for, what I wanted to be [as far as promotions are concerned]. I'm vocal in a positive way. I'm strong, not namby-pamby.

"'What do you think I need to do to get to this future job?' is a question I ask my superiors."

Henry explained that by soliciting advice, she is paving the way for the other person to "buy into" her career plans. "I make demands," she said, "but I don't threaten."

Later in the interview, she demonstrated hard language again. "As an editor," Henry explained, "I am viewed as the paper itself. People call in daily to object and I think I should talk to them."

She tells her audience what happened after her first conversation with the Kodak retiree:

"It's a story that's not going to go away. It's a major story and there's much more to be reported on it. I don't expect all of our readers to be pleased with us for reporting it. But it would be irresponsible for us not to.

"And, by the way, I invited the retired Kodak employee who called me to write something for our "Speaking Out" page. He said he would, but only if I edited it with him personally. We spent an hour in my office one day going over each sentence. We gave him half a page to take us to task, including his opinion that Frank Gannett would be appalled at his newspapers.

"Now, we're on a first-name basis. I understand Ernie a little bit better and I think he understands me a bit better even though we don't agree."

Disarm with Honesty

Henry cites her ability to be forthright as one of her most valued traits. She feels that, as a leader, she can acquire followers by disarming them with honesty. We have seen examples of this behavior in her speech. Here is another, from the beginning of her talk, in which she actually invites dialogue on controversial issues.

> "That's why I chose the subject for my talk today—how newspapers have changed over the years. I know many of you are longtime Rochester residents who have seen many changes in your newspapers. Some you like, and I know, some you don't like. Maybe we can talk about some of those tonight."

Tell a Story

The value of stories and anecdotes as composites of leadership language cannot be underestimated. When Henry refers to the author of the earlier article about the Chatterbox Club, she does more than allude to his writing. She uses stories to paint a picture of a man she admires. She uses a metaphor to suggest that, like a book, he contains history within himself.

> "It was written by Henry Clune, a wonderful man and a wonderful writer. Henry is 98 years old now and just last year he came into the newspaper to have lunch with editors and reporters. He fascinated us with stories about being on the news desk the night the Titanic sunk and when the King of England gave up the throne because of his love for divorcee Wallace Simpson. He's a living history book."

Practice: Begin to collect anecdotes that will be useful in the presentations you will have to make as your career advances. If you choose to tell stories about people you have known, try to make those individuals memorable by using specific details and by finding fresh metaphors to describe them.

Establish Commonality

Bloomingdale's Department Store attributes its success to knowing the customer. The leader must know his customer, too, whether the customer is the reader of, or listener to, the words the leader has chosen. Audience analysis must be done prior to the delivery of a communication. (As Henry put it, "If you do not do your homework, you're dead.")

Use these questions to help you prepare for the important messages you will deliver. (Not all questions are applicable to every presentation you will make.)

- How much do audience members already know about the subject?
- What are their feelings about the subject?
- What are their feelings about you?
- What is the make-up of the audience?
- What are their political and/or religious affiliations?
- Is there likely to be someone who will publicly attack your position? If so, how can you anticipate and offset that attack?
- What is the age, sex, and educational level of your audience?
- How big is the audience?
- Why are they there?
- Will there be other messages preceding or succeeding your own?

With these excerpts from her address, Henry reaches out to "touch" her audience:

"You've probably heard the jokes."

"Perhaps some of you are thinking the same thing."

"You've all heard him speak to the Chatterbox Club so you know what I'm talking about."

"I started working as a reporter in the summer of 1974. You remember that turbulent time."

"Before I get into all that serious talk, I wanted to give you an example of how newspapers have changed that's closer to home. It has to do with the Chatterbox Club. I went back into our files to find out what we had written about the club and I came across a clipping from March 7, 1929."

Give a Rationale

In the course of her interview, Henry affirmed the need for leaders to disagree with the majority view if that view is an uninformed or unethical or dangerous one. "But," she asserted, "if you disagree, you have to tell why." She asked her audience that evening questions that they probably wanted to ask her, and ended with:

"And probably the granddaddy question of them all—Why don't you cover the issues?"

Of course, she was prepared to answer that question.

"Now, the question about why we don't cover the issues. You know, issues are tough things for candidates. They can get in trouble when they take stands on issues. Look at Jimmy Carter. He said he would balance the budget in one term. It didn't quite work out for him.

"Walter Mondale addressed the issue of that deficit head-on by saying he would raise taxes. That didn't quite work out for him either. Campaign promises can come back to haunt the candidates, so maybe it's easier for George Bush to call Michael Dukakis a card-carrying member of the American Civil Liberties Union and for Dukakis to say Bush is soft on drugs because of the problems with Panama's Manuel Noriega. Then they don't have to deal with real issues."

"Coverage of elections in newspapers has changed because candidates carefully avoid questioning from the press. They issue position papers instead of answering direct questions. They carefully set up the system for the debates so they can avoid answering a question.

"They cater to TV because they know that if they get 60 seconds free on the evening news, it saves them hundreds of thousands in advertising costs. And it's easier to get on the evening news by making quick, clever comments about patriotism and the Pledge of Allegiance than it is to discuss in detail your plan to cut the deficit.

"All this isn't to say that we can't do a better job of covering elections. Of course we can. It's just some information to give you an idea of what we're up against."

Use an Attention-Getter

The place for attention-getters is either at the beginning of the presentation or at the end (and, of course, any place in-between). Use attention-getters to hook your audience into actively wanting to hear or read your message. We saw that Henry used humor at the beginning of her remarks. Your own strategy might include some of these other popular attention-getters:

- Citing an impressive statistic
- Using an anecdote
- Quoting a famous person
- Establishing a commonality with the audience
- Asking a question
- Using a deductive approach by stating your purpose immediately.

Practice: What attention-getting openings (or closings) have impressed you in the recent memos and/or presentations you have been exposed to? Begin to compile a list of effective attention-getters that you might use in your future communications.

Be Outspoken—within Reason

Henry was asked to specify the determinants of her success. "I'm ambitious, flexible, and have always been willing to move," she replied. "I work hard," was her comment. "You cannot fake it in the newspaper business because ten times a day, you are putting something out that says, 'This is what we have done!'"

Common sense is one of the most important success factors of all, she maintains. And common sense would dictate remaining calm and reasonable in potentially volatile situations.

Kitty D'Allesio, president of Chanel, Inc., once observed, "I like people who say what they mean and aren't afraid of consequences. I particularly like strong people who do things in a civilized way rather than a bullying way. I love criticism that is enriching. I don't like personal assaults." Her words can be used to describe the way Barbara Henry deals with both criticizers and conditions that deserve criticism.

The next chapter deals with the words of Kitty Carlisle Hart, one of America's best-known entertainers. In her address to the New York City Planning Commission, she touches some of the same chords sounded by Pat Russell, former president of the Los Angeles City Council. The words of both women will be examined in our final consideration of the language of leadership.

Practice: The first few paragraphs of Drucker's column are explicated here; the elements of leadership language have been identified. After reading the selection, practice identifying other elements to be found in the whole passage, which continues on the next page.

Here are some of the elements to look for: questions, repetition, parallelism, stories, metaphor, variety in sentence length, definition, an ending that ties in to the beginning, inspiration, hard words, alliteration, personification.

THE 10 RULES OF EFFECTIVE RESEARCH
by Peter F. Drucker

attention-getting introduction

variety in sentence structure

Some businesses—not very many—get a fiftyfold, or even a hundredfold, return on the research dollar. Many more get little or nothing. The key to success is not knowledge, intelligence or hard work—and least of all, luck. It is following the 10 Rules of Effective Research.

format via enumeration

radical ideas

1. Every new product, process or service begins to become obsolete on the day it first breaks even.

transition

2. Thus, your being the one who makes your product, process or service obsolete is the only way to prevent your competitor from doing so.

strong opinion

specific example to substantiate points

familiar language

One major American company that has long understood and accepted this is Du Pont Co. When nylon came out 50 years ago, Du Pont immediately put chemists to work to invent new synthetic fibers to compete with nylon. It also began to cut nylon's price—thus making it less attractive for would-be competitors to find a way around Du Pont's patents. This explains why Du Pont is still the world's leading synthetic-fiber maker, and why Du Pont's nylon is still in the market, and profitably so.

(THE 10 RULES OF EFFECTIVE RESEARCH, Continued)

A Meaningless Distinction

3. If research is to have results, the 19th-century distinction between "pure" and "applied" research better be forgotten. It may still work in the university, but in industry it is meaningless, if not an impediment. A minor change in machining a small part, for example, may require pure research into the structure of matter. Yet creating a totally new product or process may involve only careful re-reading of a standard handbook. Nor is pure research necessarily more difficult than re-defining a problem so that well-known concepts can be applied to its solution.

4. In effective research, physics, chemistry, biology, mathematics, economics and so on are not "disciplines." They are tools. This does not mean, of course, that effective research requires universal geniuses. The most brilliant physicist or chemist today knows only a small corner of his own discipline. But effective research demands that the project leader or research director know when to call on what specialist. The best example may be the way in which Jim Webb, President Kennedy's head of NASA in the 1960s, mobilized a dozen different disciplines to put a man on the moon. Mr. Webb was not a scientist but a lawyer-accountant.

5. Research is not one effort—it is three: improvement, managed evolution, and innovation. They are complementary but quite different.

   - Improvement aims at making the already successful better still. It is a never-ending activity that requires specific quantitative goals, such as annual improvements of 3 percent or 5 percent in cost, quality and customer satisfaction. Improvement starts with feedback from the front line: people who actually make the product or deliver the service; sales people; and, vitally important, the users. Then the company's own scientists, engineers or product designers must convert the front line's suggestions and queries into changes in product, process or service.

The best-known practitioners of continuing improvement today are the Japanese. Its inventor and most consistent practitioner, however, was an American company, the Western Electric subsidiary of the old Bell Telephone System.

- Managed evolution is the use of a new product, process or service to spawn an even newer product, process or service. Its motto is "each successful new product is the stepping stone to the next one."

The best-known practitioner is probably Sony, which has systematically evolved a dozen new products—the Walkman, for instance—out of the original tape recorder. But the most successful practitioner is probably a "no-tech" American business, ServiceMaster Co. of suburban Chicago, a multibillion-dollar multinational doing business successfully in the U.S., Japan and Western Europe. ServiceMaster started with the systematic application of industrial engineering to hospital maintenance and the training of low-skill people. It then evolved this, step by step, into office maintenance, factory maintenance, home maintenance and the care of elderly shut-ins. Managed evolution is always market-driven; it often requires, however, new, or at least newly developed, technology and tools.

- Innovation, finally, is the systematic use as opportunity of changes in society and the economy, in demographics and technology.

The key to effective research is to pursue improvement, managed exploitation and innovation simultaneously though separately. The classic example is again Du Pont's strategy in synthetic fibers. As I mentioned earlier, the company immediately began work on inventing competing fibers. But it also immediately started to improve nylon and to pursue managed evolution. Nylon was developed for women's stockings. But soon it was modified to serve as automotive tire cord— probably the most profitable application for many years.

The first five rules are about what to do. The last five lay down how to do it.

6. Aim high! Trivial corrections usually are as hard to make and as staunchly resisted as fundamental changes. Successful research asks: If we succeed, will it make a real difference in the customer's life or business? The Japanese control the market in videotape recorders and fax machines, both American inventions, because they set higher research goals than any American company thought attainable—in terms of product size, performance and price.

7. Yet, effective research requires both long-range and short-range results. The efforts needed are too great to be satisfied with the short-term alone. A short-term result must also be a step in a continuing long-term process. The needed balance is difficult to design. But it usually can be attained by retrospective analysis.

Researchers have long known that they should go back and read their own lab notes. Did anything happen that was pushed aside because it was unexpected or because it did not seem to lead toward the desired research objective? If so, was it actually an indication of an opportunity? Above all, was it an indication of a usable and useful short-term result? The best-known example is how Alexander Fleming came to realize that he had stumbled upon penicillin but had thrown it away as spoiling his bacterial cultures. In improvement, where results by definition are short-term, one looks for the long-term implications. One analyzes the work of the past two or three years with this question: Did successful improvements cluster around one particular application, one particular market, one design, one process, one product? This often indicates an opportunity for fundamental, long-term innovation or change.

One large company that seems to have mastered this balancing act is Merck, one of the world's largest pharmaceutical companies. Another is the medical-electronics business of General Electric. While working on such radical innovations as body scanning and nuclear magnetic resonance imaging, it has systematically fed back from these major long-term innovations to make constant, immediate improvements in its conventional X-ray apparatus.

8. Research is separate work, but it is not a separate function. Development—the translation of research results into products, processes and services that can be manufactured, sold, delivered and serviced—must go hand in hand with research. And manufacturing, marketing and service all affect research from the beginning, just as much as the results of research in turn affect them. In the university, research may be the search for new knowledge as an end in itself. In industry, in government and in medicine, research is the search for new utility.

9. Effective research requires organized abandonment—not only of products, processes and services, but also of research projects. Every product, process, service and research project needs to be put on trial for its life every few years, with this question: Would we now start this product, process, service, or research project, knowing what we know now?

Three good clues to when to abandon:

First, when there are no more significant improvements. Second, when new products, processes, market, or applications no longer come out of managed evolution. Third, when long years of research produce only "interesting" results.

Reviewing Innovations

10. Research has to be measured like everything else. For improvements, it is fairly easy to set specific goals and to measure them. In managed evolution, too, goals can be set—e.g., one new significant product, market or application every year. Innovation, however, requires appraisal. Every three years or so a company needs to review its innovative results. What did we innovate that made a difference in the wealth-producing capacity of this company? Were these innovations commensurate in numbers, quality and impact with our market standing and our leadership position in our industry? What will our innovation results have to be in the next few years—again, in numbers, quality and impact—to give us the market standing and industry leadership we need?

   Research expenditures in American business—flat or even declining the past few years—are starting to climb again. But spending money does not by itself guarantee results. Applying the 10 Rules of Effective Research does.

CHECKLIST

☐ Have I attempted to warm up or invite my audience to continue listening to my message?

☐ Have I used an attention-getter?

☐ Have I used transitions?

☐ Have I expressed strong opinions?

☐ Have I avoided sexist language?

☐ Have I used hard language?

☐ Is there evidence of concrete examples?

☐ Have I aligned metaphors with the values or traits of the audience?

☐ If appropriate, have I disarmed my audience with honesty?

☐ If a story could be used to make a point, have I used it?

☐ Did I establish common ties to my audience?

☐ Have I done my homework on the make-up of the audience?

☐ Have I provided a sound rationale for a strong stand I took or a negative response I had to give?

Footnotes

[28] Drucker, Peter F., "The 10 Rules of Effective Research," *The Wall Street Journal*, May 30, 1989. p. A16. Reprinted by permission of *The Wall Street Journal*. Copyright © 1989. Dow, Jones & Co., Inc. All rights reserved.

CHAPTER EIGHT:
The Language of Activism:
A Study of Kitty Carlisle Hart's Words

Speech was made to open man to man, and not to hide him; to promote commerce, and not to betray it.

David Lloyd

Introduction

Kitty Carlisle Hart is a woman who has worn many hats in her lifetime—each of them fetching, each of them designed to entertain or aid others: television panelist, author, singer, stage actress and movie star (she was the ingenue in the Marx Brothers' classic, *A Night at the Opera*). She is also known, of course, as the wife of one of the world's most beloved playwright/directors, Moss Hart.

Her current "hat" is that of activist for the arts: she is Chairman for the New York State Council on the Arts. As such, she is called upon to make presentations to a wide array of audiences, many of them legislative or civic in nature.

In our examination of the remarks she made to the New York City Planning Commission, we shall also use her address as a framework. With this framework, we shall summarize the various components of leadership language that we have found used by the other leaders studied in this book.

In the aggregate fabric of this language we find similar threads. We shall label these threads the "10-C Approach" as we study them one by one in the pages that follow. (Although many of the "C"s in the 10-C approach apply equally to spoken and written communication, we shall inspect them from the perspective of the speech Kitty Carlisle Hart delivered.)

An effective communicator is able to align her subject and her audience. She gives proof that her topic affects them and in so doing secures their interest. People will listen to what impacts their lives.

Before inspecting how Hart has made this alignment, here are a few tips that will help you to get started the next time you have an important communication to prepare.

Techniques for Getting Started

1. *The explosion-implosion technique.*

The brain is taking in stimuli at an incredible rate of speed. Harness this mental energy with the following getting-started technique: Draw a circle in the center of a clean sheet of paper. Inside the circle, write one or two key words that represent the focus of your document or speech. Then let your brain go wild, generating ideas related to the focus. Let each of these ideas radiate outward, like the spokes from the hub of a wheel.

"Explode" in this fashion for up to five minutes. Then go in to the "implosion" stage; begin to refine the scribbled ideas that were exploding inside your head. Pull the disparate pieces of thought into a refined whole by discarding some, combining others, rearranging the concepts in priority fashion.

2. *The topical technique.*

For your next speech or lengthy document, brainstorm the four or five major topics on which the communication should be based. Then list subordinate ideas under each of these major headings.

3. *The collection technique.*

If you have the advantage of knowing well in advance that a particular speech or report is expected of you, you can begin to collect, over a period of several weeks, ideas, quotations or observations.

Don't hesitate to ask others their views on the issue you will be addressing. If you can, do some reading on the topic. Let the thoughts incubate in your brain for a while.

Then, when your file begins to bulge, or when your deadline is two weeks away, look over all these thoughts and begin to assimilate them into the body of your speech or report.

4. *The stream-of-consciousness technique.*

In a true James-Joycean fashion, just start writing—whatever comes into your head. Even if your sentences are not directly related to the topic at hand, continue writing. Sooner or later, your thoughts will return to the subject and you will be able to relate them to the points that need to be made. Write fast, as the ideas will be spilling forth quickly. Do not stop to edit or to worry about spelling or grammar.

Practice: You have to practice a new concept every day for at least two weeks before it becomes part of your normal behavioral pattern. Start right now with the explosion-implosion technique. Take out a clean sheet of paper and write the key word(s) in the center of a circle—for example, the word "quality." Then explode with ideas related to this concept for a few minutes. Afterwards, implode those ideas into a cohesive whole. Practice this daily.

If you are not scheduled to make a significant presentation in the next several weeks, you can nonetheless begin to collect ideas and sayings and newspaper clippings about a topic that interests you. Commit to preparing a brief presentation on that topic by the end of next month. Submit your communication either to the company newsletter or to a trade journal, or deliver your presentation to the local Toastmasters Club or to a group in your area who would be interested in your topic. (Remember that George Bernard Shaw practiced such voluntary speeches several times a week for twelve years before becoming one of the world's greatest debaters.)

Assume you have to prepare a memo announcing the appointment of your boss to a special Presidential Commission. Use the stream-of-consciousness technique to prepare the points you would like to make in this announcement.

Here, then, is the outline for the first three C's of speech preparation:

Beginning

1st "C"	—	**Compliment**
2nd "C"	—	**Citing the occasion**
3rd "C"	—	**Commonality**

1st "C"—Compliment

Hart begins quite simply enough. "Thank you, Bob. I'm honored to be here this morning." The word "honored" suggests this was not an ordinary occasion for her. Every person alive loves to hear praise and this technique of complimenting the audience works well.

Hart embellishes upon her compliment by citing specifics about the city of New York. There is poetry in these pride-instilling words. The word "honored" is often used as an opening line. The poor speaker does not explain the source of that honor. By contrast, Hart brings sincerity to the word by describing exactly why it is an honor to represent that city in one capacity or another. (Note the parallelism in her sentence structure.)

"It is not hyperbole to say that it is the richness and the diversity of the arts in New York City that distinguish this city from all others. The arts soften the city's hard edges, the arts appeal to what is best in our character. The arts, frankly, make us want to live here."

Let us turn to the words of Pat Russell, former (and first woman) president of the Los Angeles City Council. Russell has assumed a leadership position in both regional and city government and political organizations. She begins her remarks at a fundraising event in an unusual way:

> "Thank you for being here. You are wonderful. I'm glad to be here."

By stressing the "you" attitude instead of the "I" attitude, Russell displays the same kind of sincerity and concern for others that we have already seen in the opening lines of the Hart speech.

Practice: Prepare an introduction which employs the 1st "C." Compliment your audience in a way that sounds sincere. Use specific details to refer to a source of mutual pride.

Cognizant of the need to get directly to the point, Hart reaches her subject matter immediately. Today's audiences, after all, do not have the temporal luxuries of an earlier generation. Life moves rapidly today—too rapidly perhaps. Waves of information lap at the shorelines of our lives every second, sometimes threatening to drown us in a sea of knowledge.

Hart wastes neither time nor words. By the third sentence, she has already established her theme:

> "As Chairman of the New York State Council on the Arts, I think no theme could be more appropriate than 'The Challenge Ahead,' and I'd like to address my comments to the challenges—and the opportunities—that I see ahead of us through the coming decade."

2nd "C"—Citing the Occasion

Within the first paragraph of her remarks, Hart speaks of feeling privileged to be "participating in the celebration of the 50th anniversary of the New York City Planning Commission."

This second "C" has value for virtually any speech. There is usually a reason why people have gathered to hear a speaker and that reason can be used to establish good will and friendly relations with your audience. Diverse as your audience is, they will share at least one thing in common: the fact that for a few moments in the long stretch of their lives, they are together to share time and space for a specific purpose. Capitalize upon that purpose by citing the occasion for their convening.

If you will turn to page 103, you will find several references to the occasion of inauguration in the speech of former President Reagan, the first of which occurs in the second paragraph:

> "This is, as Senator Mathias told us, the 50th time that we the people have celebrated this historic occasion. When the first President, George Washington, placed his hand upon the Bible, he stood less than a single day's journey by horseback from raw, untamed wilderness. There were 4 million Americans in a Union of 13 states. Today, we are 60 times as many in a Union of 50 states."

Hart has cleverly taken the theme of the occasion (as do Peters and Iacocca in earlier chapters) and incorporated that theme—"The Challenge Ahead"—into her own remarks.

Our most accomplished communicators adapt themselves to the occasion in order to establish familiarity with the audience and capture their attention.

Practice: Think about some upcoming event either in your company or your personal life or your community; plan remarks that refer to the occasion.

3rd "C"—Commonality

Hart reaches out to what the people in that room have in common: the fact that they are all New Yorkers. She shows how New York is unique among cities that share some aspects of metropolitan identity. And, she inserts a bit of her own history in relation to the Commission's history.

"Of course, we have a uniquely built environment and uniquely intensified social problems, ranging from homelessness and housing to mass transit and our public schools. But *each* city has its architectural heritage, *each* city has its own list of social ills and social conflicts, *each* city has its corporate headquarters.

"As New Yorkers, we have sometimes learned painfully that corporate loyalty to this city can be ephemeral; offices move back to South Dakota, New Jersey, Delaware. But none of those other cities or states can offer the range of artistic opportunities that New York does—from the Studio Museum in Harlem and the Queens Museum and the Brooklyn Academy of Music and Museum Mile to the wealth of commercial and non-commercial theater, independent film, galleries, readings of new writing, video, dance, new music and old.

"It is the arts that most relate to the question of 'quality of life' and it is the arts that make us choose to put up with the difficulties of living in this tough urban environment. I know, because I came to New York several years before this Planning Commission was even founded in order to perform on Broadway."

Russell achieves the same feeling of commonality through the use of the first-person pronouns "we" and "our" in the following:

"The solutions needed are not mysterious. [This is the same assertion Judith Bardwick made in her presentation.] We know what to do. The question is, do we have the skills, the will and the courage to make the tough decisions, to sacrifice some comfort today for the health and safety of our children and the resources of the earth tomorrow?"

Practice: What are the things that unite you with your usual audience? If that audience is composed of co-workers who primarily read the things you have written, make a list of work-related ideas or purposes or equipment or missions that you share.

If that audience is composed of people from various places or firms who happen to belong to the same club or religious group or political party, make a separate list of the commonalities you could mention in your next address to them.

Use your list to develop an underlying theme for your next communication.

For the middle section of your speech, these are the "C"s on which you should concentrate:

Beginning

1st "C"	—	Compliment
2nd "C"	—	Citing the Occasion
3rd "C"	—	Commonality

Middle

4th C	—	**Concrete Examples**
5th C	—	**Comparison and Contrast**
6th C	—	**Challenge**
7th C	—	**Change**

4th "C"—Concrete Examples

The specific is always more engaging than the vague. Readers and listeners will always be more interested in hearing about "a colleague who resembles Mamie Eisenhower" than hearing about "a woman with whom you work."

Beginning a talk about the elliptical, monosyllabic style of Emily Dickinson will never intrigue an audience as much as telling them about the woman who always dressed in white and who was so shy she could only relate to neighbors via her poems, which she lowered in a basket from her bedroom window for a neighborhood child to deliver.

You can develop the middle section of your communication with the use of express details. Note how Hart affects her audience by citing specific, concrete examples such as this one.

"Our humane and caring response to people with AIDS in this city is a challenge that cannot go unheeded. This society's ability to provide adequate (and affordable) medical care and health insurance will be one way we are judged years from now. When I learned last week that one arts organization had its group health insurance dropped because of the presence of the word 'Dance' in its name, I realized we have yet to understand that we are all in this battle together."

The same concrete language is used by Russell, who lost an election after serving on the City Council for 18 years. The details of her experience cannot help but draw the audience to her.

"The reports of my demise were *not* greatly exaggerated. Losing was a bummer and I have experienced real misery. About myself, I have felt fine. I first ran for office to accomplish some goals, and I achieved far more than I ever anticipated.

"By my standards, and those of most other people, I have done a good job. My misery comes from the feeling I let my loyal and wonderful people down.

"However, during these past weeks, I have received flowers, phone calls and many letters expressing support and above all understanding. These have helped me go beyond the worry of having let people down and to realize that losing is a universal experience, though not always in so public a manner."

A concrete, rather than ambiguous or undefined message is also conveyed via enumeration. We find both women enumerating their points:

From Hart:

"(1) The future of the arts in this city will depend on our ability to provide, as a city and as a society, affordable rehearsal and performance space for arts organizations and for individual artists.

(2) Hand-in-hand with the foregoing is the question of affordable housing for artists.

(3) We must develop new ways of combining corporate, foundation and public support to ensure that non-traditional arts and smaller arts organizations which exist in all five boroughs will have an opportunity to develop and to flourish. [Interestingly enough, this theme of union is also sounded in Russell's speech: "It is my observation that where significant progress on the difficult issues facing us has been made, it is nearly always because of a partnership between local government and the private sector."]

(4) One challenge that we must address in the coming decade is that of cross-pollinating audiences.

(5) The Governor's personal interest in arts-in-education led to a new program at the Council on the Arts.

(6) Our humane and caring response to people with AIDS in this city is a challenge that cannot go unheeded.

(7) Finally, the preservation and enhancement of the quality of our daily life in New York is essential if we are to remain a welcoming home for the arts, for artists and for an arts-going public."

Certainty of organization is equally evident in Russell's comments:

"The processes of government are simply not suitable to the issues we must now resolve."

"A second major issue is the lack of a public forum for information exchange and public debate."

" A third issue is that of justice and economic equality in our system."

How else are ideas made explicit? Often by the use of parallelism. Who could deny the poignancy in this Franklin Roosevelt speech to the nation? In depicting the grimness of war, he is denying charges that have been made in Europe, charges that America is a nation of weaklings.

The use of parallel structure carries a forcefulness all its own.

> "Let them tell that to General MacArthur and his men.
> Let them tell that to the sailors who today are hitting hard in the waters of the Pacific.
> Let them tell that to the boys in the Flying Fortresses.
> Let them tell that to the Marines."

Concrete examples, written in parallel syntax, were used by Hart as she describes how it is

> "...the arts in New York City that distinguishes this city from all others.
> The arts soften the city's hard edges,
> the arts appeal to what is best in our character.
> The arts, frankly, make us want to live here."

Russell includes a similar cataloging in her words:

> "We are being crowded—as in traffic jams.
> Feeling threatened—as in crime on streets and freeways.
> Feeling poisoned—by our bay and drinking water.
> Feeling overrun—by people moving in on us from other places."

Practice: Make each of the following nouns come alive by using concrete, specific descriptors in lieu of the vague references.

Chief Executive Officer	corporate policy
file clerk	incentive
conference room	quality

For the next memo or report you have to write, enumerate the points you wish to make, devoting one whole paragraph to each idea.

5th "C"—Comparison and Contrast

Further development of the body of your document can be executed with the 5th "C," Comparison and Contrast. You can create distinct impressions for your audience by juxtaposing two similar or two different concepts.

Ronald Reagan does a masterful job of comparing Adams and Jefferson, who had become antagonists during their public service. (See page 103 of the book for the full text.) Look for the metaphors in the words of both Reagan and Jefferson.

"In 1826, the 50th anniversary of the Declaration of Independence, they both died. They died on the same day, within a few hours of each other. And that day was the Fourth of July. In one of those letters exchanged in the sunset of their lives, Jefferson wrote, 'It carries me back to the times when, beset with difficulties and dangers, we were fellow laborers in the same cause, struggling for what is most valuable to man, his right of self-government. Laboring always at the same oar, with some wave ever ahead threatening to overwhelm us, and yet passing harmless...we rode through the storm with heart and hand.'"

In her address, Russell compares her disappointment at losing the election to her current state of mind. She employs an apt metaphor for a woman who literally as well as figuratively climbs mountains.

"The truth is, I have climbed a very difficult peak, with some awfully deep valleys to cross. Now I'm here, and the view is great! As when I climb real mountains, I look around and want to ascend everything in sight. I know I will accomplish some of those goals, though I can't describe the routes right now."

The comparison and contrast method, though usually elaborated upon in a communication of any length, can actually be handled in a single sentence. Perhaps the most efficient of all comparison-contrast statements belonged to Winston Churchill in his devastating likening of himself to Sir Stafford Cripps:

"He has all of the virtues I dislike and none of the vices I admire."

Practice: Draw comparisons and contrasts between several different work-related situations. For example, you may delineate the similarities and the differences between your current position and your previous one, or between your current employer and other firms in the same industry. Make your details as precise and salient as possible.

6th "C"—Challenge

Leadership language issues challenges. The leader wins supporters and acquires followers by making others want to advance a cause or develop a concept or fulfill a mission.

To transform ordinary people into advocates for an issue means exposing them to harsh realities. We often need to have our eyes opened before we can proceed along a straight path toward our goal. In painting a bleak picture, the leader is simultaneously challenging us to pick up a figurative paintbrush and make the world a brighter place.

In discussing the need for New York to provide space for its artists, Hart reveals:

"Manhattan alone has lost 55 dance studios in the past decade and there's no indication that a turnaround is about to happen. This question of affordable space is perhaps the greatest challenge we face."

And in discoursing about the need to broaden the arts-loving base, she cites the "challenge...of cross-pollinating audiences."

"By that I mean, bringing new audiences to our minority-run programs and making our museums and arts organizations more aware of the needs of this city's so-called 'minority' populations. By establishing such a dialogue among our many artistic traditions, we can ensure audiences for all the arts in the City of New York."

Russell also issues a challenge to her audience:

"Inadequate governmental processes reinforce mindless news presentation and encourage manipulation of the media. In an era of such technological advances we label it the "great communication age," we have more noise and less communication than at any other time in history! For myself, I know I must improve my media manipulation, but for public policy, we must look to those involved with modern communications to show us new paths, and some of you are here tonight."

At another point, she states, "Let me describe some of the challenges I see."

Practice: Define a challenge you would like to tackle by presenting the bare and perhaps grim facts about the situation you feel needs to be changed. Then prepare a statement from a leadership stance, encouraging followers to join you in this challenging struggle.

7th "C"—Change

Jawaharlal Nehru asserted that "the basic fact of today is the tremendous pace of change in human life." In the nearly 30 years since his death, his words have acquired even greater relevance. The leader knows change is upon us every moment of our lives. He anticipates that change and helps his followers to prepare for it.

Hart speaks of the next generation:

"This City must be able to attract the next generation of artists, and we are losing these creative people to cities like Seattle and Portland because our housing has become so extraordinarily expensive."

She forges ahead, prescribing the cure for the funding ills.

"I feel the Council on the Arts has been enlightened in its developmental role, but now, as the State faces its own budgetary problems, we must make certain that new partnerships among funding sources can support the diversity of the arts in this city."

Russell, too, speaks of the next generation:

"Will we be able to develop enough of a consensus to protect the next generation? I fear less the problem of single issues than the attitude of a whole generation which thinks only of its own time, which says, "Take away our traffic jams, tell us we don't have to worry about economic development, keep outsiders away from our houses, and then promise us that roads, jobs, and houses will be there when we need them."

As Iacocca put it, the leader must sometimes "tell people things they don't want to hear" in order to get them to "go out and do things they don't want to do."

The leader looks to the future. We see Russell here discussing issues of the next century (issues nearly identical to those being discussed by Hart on another coast).

"While president of the League of California Cities [Russell is only the second woman in the history of that influential organization to hold that title], I launched an exploratory effort to find ways to make our city governments work better, to resolve the issues of air quality, waste management, housing, transportation, human services, and to fulfill our water needs as we go into the 21st Century. It is called the "Committee of 21" and its first report has gone into its fourth printing. Those of you who haven't yet seen it should find it interesting reading."

Before turning to the 8th "C," let us review the 10-C outline and preview the remaining C's.

<table>
<tr><td colspan="3">Beginning</td></tr>
<tr><td></td><td>1st "C"</td><td>— Compliment</td></tr>
<tr><td></td><td>2nd "C"</td><td>— Citing the Occasion</td></tr>
<tr><td></td><td>3rd "C"</td><td>— Commonality</td></tr>
</table>

Beginning
    1st "C" — Compliment
    2nd "C" — Citing the Occasion
    3rd "C" — Commonality

Middle
    4th "C" — Concrete Examples
    5th "C" — Comparison and Contrast
    6th "C" — Challenge
    7th "C" — Change

End
    8th "C" — Confidence
    9th "C" — Closing
    10th "C" — Call for Action

8th "C"—Confidence

In the language of leaders you will find an expression of confidence, confidence in the ability of the followers to solve a problem or right a wrong or set a figurative ship back on its keel.

This motivational language is found near the end of the Hart speech:

"The City Planning Commission has a unique role in addressing these difficult questions from the broadest possible range of perspectives. Too often we isolate single issues, removing them from their broader context. [Her words echo the earlier quotation from Russell's speech.] But to discuss the quality of our schools is to discuss the presence of the arts in the schools; and to bring up real estate issues is to confront those questions of rehearsal and performance space. The arts pose the possibility of making our citizens aware of what we have in common and thus helping to defuse the bigotry and racism that are all too common in this city."

Listen to the inspiration coming through in this expression of confidence. In the next selection, Russell also appeals to the audience's sense of pride.

"Our city showed the world how to put on the Olympics. We have brought in water and made the desert bloom. We demonstrated early waste management with the first sanitary landfills. We produced a new transportation system called freeways. We *can move on*—the people in this room are able to put it together. I am ready to work with you, the elected, whom I know and love so well, you doers and dreamers whose visions I share. We are all 'can-do' people."

Practice: Prepare a comparable message in which you state your confidence in a group of followers to tackle a difficult situation and see it through to a successful conclusion. Appeal to their sense of pride, of competition, and of hope.

9th "C"—Conclusion

There are numerous ways to signal to your audience that you are ready to conclude. Hart does it simply with the word "finally." You may indicate you are nearly through with words such as "in summary," "to conclude," "one final comment," et cetera.

Make your conclusion memorable, punchy, climactic. The last words you speak are usually the first words your audience will remember. Some leaders like to conclude by *briefly* restating the main points of their address. Others feel that if the audience didn't absorb their points by this stage in the speech, they never will.

One good practice is to return to the theme of the evening and give it a slightly different twist. Russell mentioned hiking early in her presentation; she returns to that topic at the end. Her imagery here suggests growth and fruition and hope for the future.

"Tomorrow I will turn the compost heap, harvest some late tomatoes, schedule some climbing with Bill. Then I'll be around and I'll be seeing you."

Other means of concluding a presentation center on the attention-getting techniques that can be used in the introduction as well. For example, Judy Columbus uses a quotation from *A Chorus Line:* "Kiss today goodbye and point me toward tomorrow."

Judith Bardwick closes with a paraphrase of the Ben Franklin maxim "No pain, no gain" by saying

"That gain is worth a lot of pain."

Practice: Over the next several weeks, listen to the conclusions used by various speakers in your work environment and on the television. Begin to collect noteworthy conclusions. Which of the speakers used signal words to advise the audience of the end of the speech? What were the signal words used to prepare the audience, so they could mentally recapitulate the points made or formulate questions they would like to ask?

Which of the leaders used a restatement of their points as their conclusion? How effective were such endings? Did any of the speakers virtually restate the whole speech instead of simply the most cogent points? (There is no quicker way to lose an audience than to give a whole speech over again when you should be giving only the summary.)

Did some of the leaders employ a return to the theme with which they opened their presentations? Did you feel these circular tie-ups worked to present a tightly organized presentation?

What attention-getters were used at the conclusion? Were there some that you could use in future situations?

No leader would conclude by saying, "Well, that's it." Nor would any true appreciator of the language of leadership say something as insipid as "That's all I have to say." Such conclusions suggest a lack of preparation as well as a lack of creativity.

10th "C"—Call for Action

Effective leaders seize the opportunity to implant one final seed in the listener's mind. You will not find them wasting that opportunity with meaningless words. Nor will you find them walking off the stage while still mumbling their conclusion. Leaders make their final statement, look right at the audience for a moment and then walk off the stage with dignity.

Leaders do not admit they have forgotten some fact or figure. At this point in the presentation, no one will really care. If you *have* forgotten a key point, the conclusion is not the time to make mention of it, except with an indirect reference.

You will not find leaders apologizing. To do so suggests they were not well-prepared. If a question arises which the leader did not anticipate, he can always promise to obtain the material in question and forward it to the individual who wishes it.

Leaders use their last few minutes to make an appeal for action. They make their final pleas during these final moments of direct interaction with their audience. We find Iacocca giving a rousing "Go get 'em, Trojans!" as a climax of his address to the USC graduates.

On a more solemn note, we have Cuomo urging his listeners:

"I ask you—Ladies and Gentlemen, Brothers and Sisters—for the good of all of us—for the love of this great nation, for the family of America—for the love of God. Please, make this nation remember how futures are built."

And Hart, inspiring the members of the commission to consider the macrocosmic questions and not the single issues:

"I am not saying that this commission can establish a Utopia on the Hudson, but your work does address the bigger, more complex questions and in so doing will assure this city's pre-eminence in the culture of the nation and the world."

Practice: Examine your memos and letters from the last several weeks. Do they end with a call for action—a statement of what the reader is expected to do next? Or do they leave the reader hanging, not knowing what will occur next in the sequence of accomplishment?

Leadership language is explicit; it tells readers and listeners what the leader expects them to do. Failing to give such direction represents a failure in the leader's charge.

CHECKLIST

☐ Have I taken advantage of the techniques for getting started?

☐ Have I incorporated a sincere compliment in my opening remarks?

☐ Is there evidence of the "you" attitude and not the "I" attitude?

☐ Have I honestly tried to avoid wasting my reader's or listener's time?

☐ When appropriate, have I made reference to the occasion?

☐ Have I attempted to build rapport by finding commonalities?

☐ Do I have concrete examples in my presentation?

☐ Have I enumerated my points?

☐ Are comparisons and contrasts in the body of my communication?

☐ Have I issued a challenge to my audience?

☐ Have I made them aware of the need to change and to prepare for the future?

☐ Have I expressed confidence in their ability to do what needs to be done?

☐ Are there signal words to indicate the communication is drawing to a close?

☐ Have I made a call for action?

EPILOGUE

There is no doubt about it: we are judged by our language as much as (perhaps more than) we are judged by our appearance, our choice of associates, our behavior. Language communicates so much more than ideas; it reveals our intelligence, our knowledge of a topic, our creativity, our ability to think, our self-confidence, et cetera.

Leadership language is in a special category, but it does not represent a mysterious talent. Observers of the young Kennedy claim he was not able to hold an audience; it was only after many years and many experiences that he acquired the command, the presence that he had. The same is true of Churchill and Shaw and any number of other leaders.

No one is born being able to speak and write like a leader. However, if the desire to use language powerfully is strong enough within you, you will—in time—acquire the language of leadership.

We have presented you with successful models—leaders in the areas of business and politics and psychology and journalism and entertainment. If you have conscientiously studied their words and faithfully done the practice exercises, you will have refined your skills.

Continue to practice, every chance you get. And continue to study the language of those leaders whom you admire. Determine to sound like a leader and your determination will create the reality.

More power to you!